200 great perennials

hamlyn | all colour gardening

200 great perennials

Richard Bird

An Hachette Livre UK Company
www.hachettelivre.co.uk

First published in Great Britain in 2009 by
Hamlyn, a division of Octopus Publishing Group Ltd
2–4 Heron Quays, London E14 4JP
www.octopusbooks.co.uk

ISBN 978-0-600-61864-5

A CIP catalogue record for this book is available from the
British Library

Printed and bound in China

10 9 8 7 6 5 4 3 2 1

Note Plant sizes are given in the form height x spread. The
dimensions given in the text are a guide only. Established
plants grown in optimum conditions might achieve the
sizes shown after three to five years, but plants that prefer
full sun that are grown in shade or those that prefer partial
shade that are grown in full sun might not achieve the
heights and spreads shown. Soil fertility and type and a
garden's microclimate will also affect a plant's size.

contents

Introduction

Perennials make a garden. Other plants, such as trees and shrubs, form the permanent structures that provide interest and shape throughout the year, and annuals and biennials add splashes of colour all summer long.

Perennials, however, offer more subtle pleasures. They bring a changing palette of colours, textures and shapes to our borders throughout the seasons. Even annuals do not have the versatility of perennials, their flowers appearing in a never-changing pattern and then suddenly vanishing.

It is the constantly changing nature of perennials that make them such interesting and useful additions to our gardens. They always have something new to offer us, as first their foliage unfurls in spring and then the flowers appear in summer and on into mid- and even late autumn. Gardeners who want to be really creative can change the colours of their garden with the seasons: pastel blues and yellows in early spring; stronger blues, yellows and pinks in late spring and early summer; and then the hotter shades of yellow, orange and red to herald autumn. No one need ever get bored with a garden of herbaceous

plants, whereas most of us are thankful when we finally tear out the annuals that have bloomed unchanging, throughout summer but as the days get shorter, begin to look rather sad.

Many people are deterred from including perennials in their gardens because they think they will involve a lot of work. In fact, as long as the ground is well prepared in advance, perennials are not difficult to look after. A few minutes a day or a couple of hours a week are all that is required for a small garden. For many gardeners, those few minutes after work are a wonderful opportunity to wind down after a busy day, and as long as you are prepared to spend a regular amount of time keeping on top of the deadheading and weeding, a perennial garden is no more work than a rose bed or large lawn.

After having fallen from favour for a number of years, perennials are becoming popular with gardeners again,

Perennials provide all the colours of the rainbow.

and there is now a tremendous range of species as well as new cultivars available, not only from specialist nurseries and mail order suppliers but also from garden centres and some well-stocked DIY stores.

Choosing suitable perennials for your garden can be difficult, largely because the choice is so vast, but looking at other people's gardens with a notebook in your hand will help you decide what to include in your own garden.

The plants described in this book are just a starting point to the wonderful world of perennials.

The symbols

The following symbols have been used as a guide to the main species discussed on each page; they do not necessarily apply to the other species, cultivars or varieties described. Although all the main species described are hardy, remember that late frosts can damage the young shoots of even the hardiest of plants.

 full sun The plant will do best if it is grown where it will be in full sun for part or all of the day.

 partial shade The plant will do best if it is grown where it will be partially shaded from direct sun for all or part of the day.

 moderate water The plant does not need extra water.

 extra water The plant requires reliably moist soil or can even be grown as a pond marginal.

 hardy The plant will generally survive in winter to temperatures of -5°C (23°F).

getting started

What is a perennial?

The word 'perennial' describes something that reoccurs every year. In gardening terms this definition could apply to any plant other than annuals or biennials, but most gardeners use it in a much more limited sense.

When they talk about perennials or herbaceous perennials they are referring to the 'fleshy' plants – not trees and shrubs – that come up each year but that are not bulbs, low-growing alpine plants or tender plants. That definition may seem to exclude a lot, but in reality it includes many tens of thousands of plants, far more than any one garden could ever contain.

Perennials come in all shapes and sizes, and they provide plants for almost all situations: sun or shade; dry or damp ground; mixed or single-colour borders; round, triangular or square borders; and, most importantly, winter, spring, summer and autumn.

Perennials can be used to create unusual but beautiful combinations.

Patterns and colour can add interest to borders.

The range is so great that the garden should never be boring. Unlike annuals, perennials rarely flower for the whole summer. At first this might seem to be a disadvantage, but in fact the contrary is true: if you choose the right combination of plants your garden will be an ever-changing picture, retaining interest throughout each season and throughout each year. In theory, if you wanted, you could have a blue garden in spring, a red garden in summer, a yellow garden in autumn and a white garden in winter simply by choosing the right plants. Few people go to this extreme, but many gardeners take advantage of the versatility of perennials to create a garden that is rarely dull, even in the depths of winter.

Foliage shapes vary widely and add contrast.

It is not just for flowers that perennials are grown. The foliage adds shape and texture to a border as well as providing areas of calm. A single plant can be used to add shape, sometimes creating a focal point to draw the eye; other plants can be used to provide groundcover or a backdrop against which more dramatic plants can be seen. Perennials are, in effect, one of the most useful and pleasing of all types of plant to grow in the garden.

Getting the best from your plants

When you are planning the design of a garden or border, try not to think of plants just in terms of the colour of their flowers (see pages 14–15). There is more to them than this. The shape, colour and texture of their leaves add a lot to the overall composition and effect, as do the overall height and shape of the fully grown plants.

Foliage

Foliage can be used to add interest in its own right or to create areas of calm between, for example, areas of contrasting or vibrant flower colour.

Some plants have silvery leaves that can be used to brighten a border. Artemisias (see pages 54–5) have lovely silvery, often filigree foliage, which is attractive in its own right and is a wonderful contrast for plants with darker leaves.

The vast range of texture, shape, size and colour available among hostas (see pages 130–31) offers endless opportunities for creating telling combinations. Glossy foliage can be used to lighten a dark, shady corner as it reflects odd shafts of light. The furry white leaves of *Stachys byzantina* (see pages 220–21) make an unusual edging to the front of a border. Indeed, some gardeners like the leaves of stachys so much that they even remove the flowering shoots so that it is entirely a foliage plant.

Form

The overall shape – or form – of the plants is also important. A quick glance at an established perennial border will soon show the wide range that plants exhibit.

Some plants, such as *Lathyrus vernus* (see pages 144–5), grow into rounded hummocks, whereas others, such as kniphofias (see pages 140–41) create fountains of narrow leaves. Some, like *Echinops sphaerocephalum* (see pages 96–7), are stiff and upright, thrusting towards the sky, while others, like nepeta (see pages 172–3), flop forwards, softening edges and breaking up straight lines. These characteristics can all be used to set one plant off against the other to make an interesting scene. A border of plants that are all the same shape and that have the same habit of growth tends to be boring.

Focal points

Large plants with a strong outline can be used to create focal points – that is, something striking that draws the eye. For example, a tall plant at the bottom of a path will draw the eye down the path, while a group of large phormiums (see pages 186–7), set at regular intervals down a border, will create a rhythm down its length. You can also use focal points to draw the eye away from less attractive features – a neighbouring building, for instance.

Left: The shape and colouring of hostas add to a border's vibrancy.
Right: Spiky plants add excitement and movement, but too many can create a restless scene.

Using colour

There are few gardeners who grow nothing but perennials, and most mix them with some shrubs, bulbs, annuals or tender plants. There are, of course, some gardeners who become so smitten by one group of plants that they grow masses of, say, geraniums, hostas or daylilies to the exclusion of practically everything else.

Even these gardeners, however, tend to mix their favoured genera with other plants, because a bed of nothing but, say, geraniums could be dull, even allowing for the great differences that exist between individual variants. However, while it creates a more interesting border to use a range of plants, it's best to avoid using too many, otherwise your garden will have a spotty, restless appearance. Large drifts of a single colour tend to be more soothing to the eye.

The way colour is used is something that interests many gardeners. Some prefer to 'paint' a picture in the garden, using soft pastel colours – pinks, pale yellows and delicate blues and mauves – to give a misty effect, which can be calming and peaceful.

Hot colours can create a sense of excitement.

Purples add a sense of calm, but can become leaden if overused.

Hot colours, such as bright golden-yellows, oranges and reds, on the other hand, are much more vibrant and tend to be exciting, but they can create a rather fevered, restless atmosphere. Do not overuse them, because the effect of these vivid colours becomes tiring after a while, rather like going to a party every night, rather than just occasionally. If you really like reds, oranges and yellows, group them but don't use too much foliage as this will make the effect seem very spotty and lose impact.

Basing an entire border or even a whole garden on a single colour can be great fun. White is a favourite choice, and there are plenty of white-flowered plants to choose from, and there are also several plants with silver or silver-variegated leaves. Creating a design based on blue or red flowers is also perfectly possible, although it's important to remember that some pinky reds don't go very well with orangey reds.

If you have a large area to plant it is perfectly possible to create a changing sequence of colours that will take you through the year, perhaps starting with soft yellows and pinks in spring, passing through brighter yellows and blues in summer, to strong oranges and reds in autumn.

15

Choosing a style

If you enjoy being in the garden and love plants, there is a great danger that you will simply buy what you like or think might be interesting and find space for it, rather than integrating your new plants into an overall scheme.

All gardens, especially small ones, will benefit if you have a clear idea of the sort of style you want and the overall effect you want to achieve.

Cottage gardens

It would be wrong to think that this traditional style of garden has gone out favour. In fact, it is making something of a comeback now that increasing numbers of people want to grow their own vegetables and herbs but do not have either the space or the inclination to have a separate vegetable garden.

This type of garden frequently appears to be a rather higgledy-piggledy jumble of colours, textures and shapes. Traditionally, there was no actual design to such a garden: plants were often just put into the ground where there was a space. In many cases, plants self-seeded and were left to crop up all over the place, creating a satisfying tapestry of colour, shapes and textures.

Cottage gardens tended to use what we now call old-fashioned plants, ones that were generally hardy and not particularly prone to pests and diseases. Since time was often at a premium, plants had to be tough enough to look after themselves. This does not mean that the plants are boring, far from it – many of them still form the backbone of our perennial plantings.

Herbaceous borders can be colour themed.

Herbaceous borders

Another traditional but more formal scheme was the long herbaceous border, often on either side of a wide, grassed path. These needed quite a bit more upkeep than a cottage garden because the plants were kept much more under control and were often planted in carefully planned drifts, with shorter plants at the front and taller ones at the back. A well-designed herbaceous can look wonderful, but there is a danger that it will look scrappy if the colours are too mixed up.

Bog gardens

Bog gardens, created on the edge of ponds or beside natural or artificial streams, can be extremely effective and attractive. They are particularly

Cottage garden plants often give a romantic feel.

interesting because you can grow plants there that will not thrive elsewhere in the garden. If you are planning to include a pond in your garden, use the opportunity to create a bog garden next to it.

Woodland gardens

Shade is often regarded as a problem in gardens, but there is a large number of plants that will not only tolerate but will thrive in shade. A woodland garden, created under deciduous trees and shrubs, can be a thing of great beauty and tranquillity and often makes a good place to sit and relax. The side of a house facing away from the midday sun provides enough shade to make a good substitute woodland garden.

Preparing the ground

Perennials tend to remain in the soil for several years, so it is essential that the ground into which they are planted is prepared thoroughly. An ill-prepared or rushed bed can result in years of problems and poor flowering.

Weeds

One of the most important tasks is to remove all perennial weeds, such as bindweed and couch grass. If the soil is light and friable (crumbly) you can often dig out the weeds by hand. If, on the other hand, it is heavy and sticky it can be almost impossible to get them out, and then your only recourse may be to use a herbicide. Used properly, this should enable you to clear the ground in one go, and ideally you will never need to use one again, so no lasting harm is done. Once the border is planted never use weedkillers.

If you don't want to use chemicals, you can try and smother the weeds with heavy-duty black polythene. It's best to work on small areas at a time, but it takes a long time to remove all the weeds – one or two months for annual weeds and at least one growing season for perennial ones – and it is not always totally effective.

Enriching the ground

Dig over the border, mixing in plenty of well-rotted organic material, such as garden compost or farmyard manure. If it is very wet you may have to install some form of drainage system, which can be expensive. If it is just sticky clay, add some horticultural grit, which, together with the organic material, will help break down the soil, and over the years it will become good quality loam.

Adding a mulch of well-rotted organic material every year will eventually transform both heavy clays and open, chalky, quickly draining soils into the type of moisture-retentive, humus-rich ground in which most perennials will not only thrive but multiply.

Phasing the work

If you are intending to plant in autumn, then do the weed clearance and digging in spring; do it in the autumn for spring planting. This time delay not only allows

soil to break down due to the action of the weather, but it allows any pieces of weed that have escaped to make themselves seen so that you can remove them before you start planting. Use a rake to level the ground and to

Well-rotted organic material added to the soil is a requirement for a good herbaceous border.

break down the soil into a tilth (a layer of fine, crumbly soil), and it is ready for planting.

Planning and planting

Some gardeners like to plan a garden on paper before they start planting. You don't have to be able to draw to do this – indeed, no one else need ever look at it, so it doesn't matter what it looks like.

If you can, outline the border or area that you want to plant up roughly to scale, then draw rough circles for the plants, indicating how big they will eventually grow. Use coloured pencils so you get a rough idea of how the colours will work. Bear in mind that the plants will flower at different times, so not all the colours will show at the same time.

Other gardeners prefer to arrange the border simply by arranging the pots containing the plants on the border and then shuffling them around until the arrangement satisfies them.

Both method needs a bit of imagination to see the border in full growth, but that is half the fun of creating a border. Whichever method you use, it is inevitable that some plants will end up in the wrong place and will need moving once they have grown to full size.

One of the most important points to remember when you're planning a border is that plants often have preferences as to where they grow. Some prefer shade and will not do well in full sun, while others grow happily in the damp margins of a pond but will languish and often die in drier parts of the garden.

Before planting do a final check that no perennial weeds have reappeared. If they have dig them out. Position all the plants so that you can make sure that the spaces are correct. Loosen the soil around where the plant is to go and work in a handful of bonemeal, then dig a hole and put in the plant. Most plants should be planted to the same depth as they were in the pot. Fill in around the plant, firm the soil down and then water.

Work from the back of the border to the front, forking out footprints and raking over as you go. If the soil is wet work on a plank to prevent compaction of the soil.

Careful planning and planting will ensure that the plant is off to a good start.

Looking after your plants

Planting is just the first stage in looking after your plants. Throughout the growing season and beyond you need to support, water and feed your plants so that they reward you with the best possible display of flowers and foliage.

Staking

It is inevitable that some plants will need support. Many gardeners plant their borders tightly so that one plant supports its neighbour, but even this approach fails in windy areas. The key to supporting plants is to make certain that the supports are hidden, which means putting them in before the plant gets too big. If you try supporting a plant once it has flopped over it will never look natural.

Aim to put in supports when the plant is only about a quarter to a third of its eventual height. The support itself should be above the growth at this point so that the plant grows through it. This way it will look natural and hide the supporting structure.

There are several types of support. Single sticks or canes can be used for tall plants such as delphiniums. These are difficult to hide and should be placed behind the plant. Hoops and linked stakes can be positioned around the growing plant. Those that have cross-wires are best because they spread the weight. A similar system can be create by placing canes around the plant and then weaving a cat's cradle of strings across the plant, forming a mesh.

If you are lucky enough to have access to peasticks, several of these can be stuck into the ground around the plant and then the top half of the stems turned at right angles across the plants and intertwined, tying if necessary, so they form a mesh of twigs through which the plant will grow. For larger drifts of plants a similar arrangement can be made by supporting large-holed wire netting on sticks just above the area of plants, so, again, the plants will grow through the mesh and are supported by it.

Vulnerable plants should always be staked before they reach full height.

Weeding

Probably the most important job in looking after a perennial border is to keep it weeded. Even though you cleared the ground before you planted anything, because your perennials will remain in position for several years, in some cases almost for ever, it is important that they do not become infested with weeds, because it will be impossible to get them out. Always weed borders by hand. Do not use a hoe because you are almost certain to chop off parts of plants or emerging shoots. Hoeing can also damage shallow roots. Do not use chemical weedkillers on an established border because no matter how still the day seems, fine spray will always manage to drift on to precious plants and either kill or disfigure them.

Start weeding early in the year, preferably in late winter. If it is left much later the weeds will start growing fast and can be difficult to keep under control. One hour spent weeding in winter can save hours later in the year.

Applying 10 cm (4 in) deep mulch of a biodegradable material such as bark, leafmould or shreddings over clean, damp soil will help keep the weeds from germinating.

Always hand-weed in a border as hoeing and spraying can cause damage to plants.

Deadheading

Most plants benefit from being deadheaded once the flowers fade. This not only makes the border look neater, but it allows you to see the remaining flowers more clearly. It also enables the plant to direct its energy into putting on new growth rather than expending the great amount of energy that is required to turn a flowerhead into seed.

Clearing away old growth

At the end of autumn most gardeners clear away all old growth by cutting the stems as close to the ground as possible. Some gardeners, however, prefer to leave the dead stems and foliage until spring both to protect the crown and so that birds and other wildlife can find a refuge or seeds and insects. The drawbacks of this approach are that pests and diseases can overwinter in the debris – it's an ideal habitat for slugs – and if the spring is wet and it's impossible to get into the borders it's all too easy to damage the new growth when you are cutting away the old dead material.

Protect the crowns of plants like gunneras (see pages 120–21) with the old leaves, holding them in place with stones or soil. You can protect the crowns of other tender plants with a mulch of bracken or straw.

Watering

Watering plants is becoming more and more of an ethical question. In fact to the perennial grower it can be less of a problem as most plants can tolerate a certain amount of drought, particularly if you have dug plenty of well-rotted compost or manure into the soil to make it more moisture-retentive and if you apply a thick mulch to the surface while the soil is damp. The mulch will prevent surface moisture from being evaporated from the soil and enable the soil to hold enough moisture for a greater part of the summer, helping the plants through drier periods.

Most plants will need watering when they are first planted and, if the weather is dry, regularly thereafter until their roots spread out into the soil.

Apart from this, however, it is generally possible to let the plants look after themselves. If you do water, the plants' roots tend to develop near the surface and they will then suffer badly if this area dries out. Not watering encourages the roots to delve more deeply where there are greater reserves of moisture.

It is rarely necessary to water the whole border but, if you decide you really must, make certain that you do it thoroughly — a trickle of water is useless. You must give enough water — at least an 2.5 cm (1 in) — for it to soak right into the ground. Water in the evening so that the plants have time to drink up the moisture before it evaporates in the heat of the next day.

Feeding

Digging in well-rotted organic material when you prepare the ground will help to feed the plants naturally. In spring topdress the border by applying a layer at least 5 cm (2 in) deep of the same well-rotted material and this will not only help as a mulch (retaining moisture and repressing weeds) but also gradually feed the soil as it breaks down. In spring it is often helpful to spread a slow-release fertilizer, such as bonemeal, around the plants, but this isn't necessary if you top dress with well-rotted organic material.

Only water if necessary and then do it thoroughly.

Propagation

There is something rather exciting about propagating plants. You start with what looks like dried dust or a bit of twig and before you know it, these tiny seeds and cuttings have transformed themselves into beautiful living plants.

Anybody can do this with patience and a little effort. The key thing to remember is that the aftercare – once the seed is up or the cutting has rooted – requires as much, or more, attention. Pot up the young plants individually as soon as possible and keep them watered, but not overwatered. Harden them off before planting out if they have been raised under glass. (To harden off plants give them access to the open air for a couple of hours on the first day, gradually increasing the amount of time each day for three or four days until they are in the open all the time.)

Seed

In general, perennial seeds are best sown as soon as you get them, and you should check the advice on the back of the packet about sowing timing, germination time, spacing and aftercare, but if you're in doubt sow half the packet when you get it and the other half in mid-spring. Some seeds, particularly of plants that flower late in the year, require a period of cold before they will germinate, and if you are collecting your own seed from plants, bear this in mind and sow the collected seed in containers that are left outdoors over winter.

Sow the seeds thinly into pots of proprietary seed compost. Do not use garden soil, which may contain pests and diseases. Cover the seeds with a thin layer of horticultural grit. Water carefully and transfer to a shady place until the seed germinates. Don't forget to label the pots. If you have one you can put the pots in a warm propagator, but most perennial seeds will germinate at ordinary temperatures.

Prick out the seedlings into individual pots as soon as the second set of leaves appear. Handle the

Sow seeds in seed compost, not garden soil.

young plants carefully, holding them by the leaves, not the roots.

Some seeds, such as those of peonies (see pages 176–7), have a long dormancy and may not appear until the second year. Do not despair if the seed does not immediately germinate.

Division

This method of propagation is very useful for perennials, although not all perennial plants can be divided. Some plants develop taproots (long, tapering roots), which do not lend themselves easily to division.

Division is ideal for plants that develop a fibrous root system, such as asters (see pages 58–9) and phloxes (see pages 184–5). Dig up the plant, wash the soil from the roots and gently pull the plant apart. Many will easily divide into individual plants. If the roots are especially tangled, you may need to cut them into sections. Make sure there is at least one growing point on each new plant. Replant these divisions in pots or, if they are large enough, back into the ground.

The crude method of wrenching plants apart with forks or even cutting them into chunks with a spade works, but it

Dividing with a spade can damage plants; hand division is preferred.

damages a lot of the roots and can allow infection to enter the plant.

Cuttings

Not all perennials can be increased by cuttings, particularly those that have a single stem, but a surprising number can. Basal cutting are taken from the young growth you can find around the base of the plant in spring or from the regrowth that shoots later in the year if a plant is cut back.

Remove a shoot about 8 cm (3 in) from the base and then trim off all the leaves except the top pair. Put the cuttings into a pot filled with sandy compost. They tend to root better if you arrange them around the edge of the pot. There is rarely need to use a rooting compound. You can put up to 12 cuttings, depending on their size, in a 9 cm (3½ in) pot. Place the pot in a propagator or even in a clear plastic bag, as long as you make sure the leaves don't touch the plastic.

Some plants, such as penstemons (see pages 180–81), can be propagated from tip cuttings taken from the tops of longer growth, using the same method. When roots appear, pot up each plant individually.

Pests and diseases

Many new gardeners worry unduly about pests and diseases. In fact, apart from slugs and occasionally greenfly (aphids), they rarely cause any problems in the garden, and you can take steps to avoid problems arising.

First, buy healthy plants from reputable sources so that you do not import problems into your garden. Second, look after your plants, feeding and watering them regularly as needed. Poorly growing plants are susceptible to diseases that have no or little affect on strongly growing ones.

The greater the range of plants you grow the better. You will attract a wide range of insects, both good and bad, and they tend to balance each other out. When you apply chemicals you kill as many good as bad insects, and then, if there is a sudden influx of harmful ones, you will have lost the battle. Many pests and diseases attack specific genera, and the greater the number of species you grow, the less likely you are to be troubled by pests and diseases. There is no need for chemicals in most gardens.

Aphids are generally only a nuisance when they reach this stage of infestation.

Pests

Two pests that are becoming more widespread are lily beetles (red insects and grubs that affect fritillaries as well as all lilies) and vine weevils, the yellowish grubs of which are a particular problem in containers because they eat a plant's roots. There are no effective chemicals available to the gardener, even though some claim to be. Remove by hand any you see and tread on them.

Slugs and snails

The pests that you are almost certain to encounter, especially early in the season when growth is soft and lush, are slugs and snails. Slug bait is the most effective way of dealing with them but should be applied so that it cannot affect other wildlife, and dead slugs should be removed.

Nematodes watered into warm ground will help control soil-dwelling slugs, and beer traps have a limited effect. One of the best methods is to go out just after dark with a torch and pick up all the slugs and snails you can find and dispose of them as you wish. After a few evenings the population will be reduced to acceptable levels.

Aphids

Aphids, which may be green or black or another colour altogether, can be seen clustered on soft shoots. They can be removed and squashed between your finger and thumb or washed off with a jet of water.

Diseases

The most often seen diseases are rusts (reddish, yellow or brown swellings on leaves) and mildews (white powdery coating on leaves and stems). These are usually disfiguring rather than life-threatening and can be mostly ignored. Burn any plants that have virus infections, which can cause distortions and stunting.

Attacks of mildew are common but rarely cause damage.

the plants

Acanthus Bear's Breeches

Key features eye-catching ✷ imposing ✷ excellent cut or dried flowers ✷ hardy

Plant in sun or light shade in most soils

Care feed and mulch in spring; cut down flower spikes before seed falls to the ground because removing seedlings can be difficult

Propagate from seed in spring

Pests & diseases trouble-free

If you want a tall, dignified plant for a border *Acanthus spinosus* could be the plant for you. It is hard to ignore and will create a good focal point as well as adding colour and shape to your garden.

An established plant will form a large clump, 60–90 cm (2–3 ft) or more across, with flower spikes rising to about 1.5 m (5 ft). The individual foxglove-like flowers are white with a purplish hood above each one. The flower spikes, which appear in late spring and continue until midsummer, can be cut and dried, and they are excellent for flower-arranging. The large, dark green leaves have spines on the deeply cut margins.

spines and no spines

Cultivars of *A. spinosus* in the Spinosissimus Group are for masochists: although beautiful, the grey-green leaves are a mass of vicious spines. *A. hungaricus*, on the other hand, bears similar flowers spikes to *A. spinosus*, to about 1.2 m (4 ft) high, but the paler green leaves are soft and spineless.

Acanthus spinosus

Achillea Yarrow

Key features good flowers and foliage * long-lasting * can be dried * alternatives give a good colour range

Plant in sun, preferably in well-drained soil, but will grow in heavier ground

Care A. 'Moonshine' may need replacing (from cuttings) after a few years; others continue for many, many years

Propagate from basal cuttings in spring for A. 'Moonshine'; other forms by division

Pests & diseases slugs can be a nuisance when growth first appears

Achilleas are excellent for adding a touch of serenity to a border. The flat heads of yellow flowers float above the leaves for a long period from summer into autumn, and some forms, such as *Achillea* 'Moonshine', 45–60 cm (18–24 in) high, have silvery foliage, which complements the bright yellow flowers.

All achilleas look better in drifts than as individual specimens, and where there is space three, ideally five, plants will look great. As they become established the clumps grow to about 45 cm (18 in) across. The flowers can be cut and dried for winter arrangements.

up and down

There are taller forms up to 2 m (6 ft) high, such as *A. filipendulina*. 'Gold Plate' and *A.* 'Coronation Gold', which make magnificent clumps. At the other end of the scale are the cultivars of *A. millefollium*, which grow to 45–60 cm (18–24 in) high and across. The species has white flowers, but there are large number of cultivars.

Achillea filipendulina 'Gold Plate'

Agapanthus African Lily

Key features eye-catching *
easy to grow * not invasive *
hardy

Plant in sun; they will grow in
most soils

Care cut back in autumn or
spring before growth restarts

Propagate by division in
spring

Pests & diseases trouble-free

Who can resist the amazing blue heads
of the various species and cultivars of
Agapanthus? They look magnificent, whether
they are grown as a clump in the border or
in containers. In the border they create eye-
catching focal points, and container-grown
plants look wonderful on patios or on either
side of the top or bottom of a flight of steps.

The blue tubular flowers are borne in round, terminal
bunches in late summer to early autumn on leafless
stems, held high above the fountain of strap-like
leaves. The height depends on cultivar, ranging from
about 30 cm to 1.2 m (1–4 ft) or more. Most modern
forms are hardy.

blue moon

Most of the African lilies that are offered for
sale will produce blue flowers, ranging from
very pale to dark blue or violet. There are,
however, some white cultivars, such as 'White
Superior', which are perfect for a white garden
or for a mixed border.

White *Agapanthus* cultivar

Alcea Hollyhock

Key features tall and stately ∗ old-fashioned looking ∗ beautiful colours ∗ easy to grow ∗ long season

Plant in full sun, although they will tolerate a little light shade

Care in windy areas they may need staking as they reach full height

Propagate from seed sown in spring; collect your own in autumn

Pests & diseases rust; although it can be ignored, affected plants are best replaced the following year

Hollyhocks are the quintessential cottage garden plant, but they are equally popular in more formal and mixed gardens. The tall flower spires, borne in early to midsummer, come in a wide range of colours, from almost black to soft pinks and yellows. Many are also available as double flowers, which almost look like nature's powder-puffs.

Most hollyhocks are tall, growing to 2 m (6 ft) or more, but there are also shorter forms, which are ideal for small gardens and containers. They are all susceptible to hollyhock rust, however, and infected plants should be replaced with new plants grown from seed every year. This can easily be done from your own seed because each plant produces masses of it.

smaller is beautiful

The species *Alcea rugosa* has similar flowers to the many cultivars, but it is often multi-stemmed and a bit shorter, to 1.2 m (4 ft). It is valuable for smaller gardens and is frequently longer lived because it is more resistant to rust.

Alcea rosea

Alchemilla Lady's Mantle

Key features quietly attractive
* good cut flowers * excellent
groundcover * easy to grow *
hardy

Plant in sun or light shade in
virtually any soil

Care cut off the flowers just
before seed is set to prevent
seedlings from appearing

Propagate from seed sown in
autumn or spring

Pests & diseases trouble-free

Even though it's so widely grown, *Alchemilla mollis* is nonetheless a thoroughly good plant. If it has any faults it is that it does self-seed, but this is easily prevented by removing the spent flowerheads. As well as the pretty greenish-yellow flowers, borne over a long period from late spring to late summer, it also has attractively pleated foliage.

Lady's mantle can be used almost anywhere in the garden. It grows to about 45 cm (18 in) and forms a clump about the same across, and if it's used in quantity it makes excellent groundcover. The cut flowers look attractive, especially with sweet peas, and both are scented.

smaller editions

There are a number of smaller species, of which *A. conjuncta*, 40 x 23–30 cm (16 x 9–12 in), is possibly the best. Like all alchemillas, it has attractive foliage, but the silvery hairs on the back of the leaves stick out, creating a silver rim to the upper surface.

Alchemilla mollis

Anaphalis Pearl Everlasting

Key features foliage plant *
good cut and dried flowers *
easy to grow * hardy

Plant in full sun and most soils

Care remove unwanted plants
regularly; mulch

Propagate by division in
spring

Pests & diseases trouble-free

Anaphalis triplinervis is one of those plants
that is grown as much for its foliage as for
the flowers. Both the stems and leaves are
covered with grey hairs, which give the whole
plant a silvery appearance. Established plants
spread slowly to make a drift, and they are a
perfect foil for more colourful plants.

In mid- to late summer plants bear tiny, daisy-like
flowers with white petals and a small yellow centre.
They last for a long time and can be dried and used in
dried flower arrangements. The plant reaches to
45–60 cm (18–24 in) tall and about 60 cm (24 in)
across, making it ideal for a position in the mid-border.

summer snow

Although the species *A. triplinervis* is good in its
own right, the cultivar 'Sommerschnee' is even
more spectacular with its bright, white flowers,
although, at about 25 cm (10 in) high, it is
somewhat shorter. Also well worth growing is
the very similar *A. margaritacea*, particularly in its
form *yedoensis*.

Anaphalis triplinervis

Anemone Windflower

Key features graceful * long flowering season * soon forms a mature clump * easy to grow * hardy

Plant in full sun or light shade

Care feed and mulch in spring; reduce the spread by digging round the edge of the clump if a plant gets too large; keep watered in dry weather

Propagate by division in spring

Pests & diseases trouble-free

The genus is large and varied, containing plants for every type of garden, but in mixed borders the tall Japanese anemones, *Anemone* x *hybrida*, are a sheer delight. The flowers appear in late summer and continue well into the autumn. There are both single- and double-flowered forms, and they are available in various shades of pink and white.

Japanese anemones are plants for the middle to back of the border as they grow to 1 m (3 ft) or more. They spread and soon form a good-sized clump. However, some can spread too far and may need cutting back, especially on lighter soils. They are useful plants because they will tolerate both sun and light shade.

woodland delights

There are lots of anemones in addition to the Japanese ones, and one of the most delightful is the wood anemone or windflower, *Anemone nemorosa*, whose delicate white flowers brighten up the spring. It grows to about 10 cm (4 in) tall and it does best in dappled shade.

Anemone x *hybrida* 'Honorine Jobert'

Anthemis Golden Marguerite

Key features clump-forming ★ non-invasive ★ long flowering season ★ easy to grow ★ hardy

Plant in full sun, preferably in well-drained, but moisture-retentive soil; can be grown in heavier soils, although not so long-lived

Care cut back old stems to the new emerging growth in spring; feed and mulch in spring

Propagate from basal cuttings taken in spring

Pests & diseases trouble-free

Daisies can be effective garden plants, and they come in all shapes and sizes. One of the most attractive of the medium-sized species, growing to about 45–60 cm (18–24 in), is *Anthemis tinctoria* and its various cultivars. *A. tinctoria* itself has deep golden-yellow flowers, each to 3 cm (1¼ in) across, in summer, but the flowers of 'Sauce Hollandaise' are a more subtle creamy yellow.

The delightful flowers appear above dark green, filigree foliage, and they are borne for much of the summer. The plants are relatively short-lived, however, and need to be replaced every two or three years.

white alternatives

Another anthemis that is eminently worth growing is *A. punctata* subsp. *cupaniana*. This is a low-growing plant, to about 30 cm (12 in), and it has silvery foliage and white flowers with yellow centres. It is ideal for groundcover at the front of the border.

Anthemis tinctoria 'Sauce Hollandaise'

Aquilegia Columbine

Key features dainty flowers ∗ attractive foliage ∗ easy to grow ∗ sun or shade ∗ hardy

Plant in full sun or light shade in most soils

Care cut off spent flowerheads unless seed is required; mulch in spring

Propagate from seed

Pests & diseases trouble-free

This plant is sometimes known as granny's bonnet, and the reason for the name becomes evident as soon as you see the curious cap-like flowers. The dainty flowers also resemble a ballerina on tip-toe, with her arms in the air. The species, *A vulgaris*, has blue flowers, but a wide range of different coloured forms has been developed over the years, and you can now find flowers in white and in all shades of pink and red.

This delightful plant, which grows to about 60 cm (2 ft) high, flowers in late spring and early summer, and it is useful for dotting around among summer plants.

colour range

There are several other species of aquilegia that will provide a wide range of colour, including *A. viridiflora*, which has unusual green and brown flowers. Both *A. canadensis* and *A. formosa* have small red and yellow flowers, which is a wonderful combination; perfect for hot borders.

Aquilegia double cultivar

Artemisia Wormwood

Key features stunning foliage * long season * easy to grow * hardy

Plant in full sun in free-draining soil, although it will also grow in heavier soil

Care cut off the flowerheads as they appear

Propagate from basal cuttings in spring

Pests & diseases trouble-free, although occasionally attracts blackfly; squash them with your fingers or wash them off with a jet of soapy water

The great thing about most artemisias is their wonderful silvery foliage. The late-summer flowers, which are relatively insignificant, are often cut off by gardeners as soon as they appear because they can detract from the plant's overall appearance.

One of the best artemisias is 'Powis Castle', which has finely cut, bright silver leaves. You could not wish for a better foliage plant. A well-grown plant can reach 1 m (3 ft) high, although it is often much less, usually 45 cm (18 in), and about the same across. It forms a great mound of filigree foliage that acts as a foil for a wide range of colours.

more silver

A close relative but with less finely cut foliage is the western lungwort, *A. ludoviciana*, which grows to 60–90 cm (2–3 ft) high. This has slightly duller foliage – more pewter than silver – but it is still effective, and there is usually room for both in most gardens. Again, it is best without its small, brown flowers. Two of the best cultivars are 'Valerie Finnis' and 'Silver Queen'.

Artemisia 'Powis Castle'

Aruncus Goat's Beard

Key features eye-catching ∗ dual-purpose ∗ can be dried ∗ sun or shade ∗ hardy

Plant preferably in an open site, although will tolerate light shade, in most soils

Care feed and mulch in spring; cut to the ground in autumn or spring

Propagate by division in spring

Pests & diseases trouble-free

This is one of those useful dual-purpose species. For most of the summer *Aruncus dioicus* is a perfect foliage plant, and then for one brief period it produces drifts of frothy flowers.

The mid-green foliage is divided and has a delicate, fern-like appearance, and then in midsummer the large heads of creamy white flowers appear, waving in the breeze, 2 m (6 ft) or more above the ground. This is a plant for a sunny spot, but if it is grown in light shade it will bloom for longer but not quite so spectacularly. It is the perfect plant for growing near a pond or in damp, but not waterlogged ground.

finely cut

Although the foliage of *A. dioicus* is attractive, that of one of its cultivars, 'Kneifii', is even more so. This is a smaller plant, 1 m (3 ft), with very finely cut leaves, almost like filigree lace. It likes the same situation as its parent.

Aruncus dioicus

Aster Aster

Key features masses of flowers * late-flowering * wide range of colours * hardy

Plant in sun in an open position in most soils

Care feed and mulch in spring; remove plants round edge of clump if too spreading

Propagate by division in spring

Pests & diseases mildew, but this can be ignored

There are so many good plants in this genus that it is difficult to choose a single representative, but probably the most popular are the Michaelmas daisies, *Aster novi-belgii* and *A. novae-angliae*, clump-forming plants that are covered with bright daisy flowers in autumn in shades of pink, mauve, blue and white.

They vary in height from only 30 cm (1 ft) to 1.5 m (5 ft), and they can form a patch 60 cm (2 ft) or more across. This type of aster is surface rooting and can be moved, even when it's in flower, which is a useful way of adding colour to where you want it in the border at a time when other flowers have gone over.

even more spectacular

Spectacular as the Michaelmas daisies can be, one of the best asters is *Aster* x *frikartii* 'Mönch'. This produces large blue flowers over a long period from midsummer until late autumn. It is 60 cm (2 ft) tall.

Aster novi-belgii cultivar

Astilbe Astilbe

Key features brilliant flower colour * good foliage * looks good in drifts * hardy

Plant in sun or light shade in most soils, although does best in moist conditions

Care feed and mulch in spring

Propagate by division in spring

Pests & diseases trouble-free

Astilbes are useful plants if you want to have a splash of bright colour. They can be used as single specimens, but they look more impressive in groups. In midsummer the hybrids of *Astilbe* x *arendsii* produce magnificent spikes of flowers in a wide range of bright colours, from creamy white through pinks and reds to purples.

These plants will grow in sun or light shade, but they look their best when they are planted beside a pond. The heights vary according to cultivar, ranging from 45 cm (18 in) to about 60 cm (2 ft). They spread slowly to form moderate-sized clumps but are not invasive.

go smaller

There is a dwarf astilbe, *A. chinensis* var. *pumila*, which is an excellent choice for the front of a border where it can make a dense, groundcovering mat without becoming invasive. It has spikes of purplish flowers and attractive reddish-green foliage.

Astilbe cultivar

Astrantia Masterwort

Key features long-lasting flowers * forms drifts * good cut flowers * hardy

Plant in sun or light shade in any soil

Care feed and mulch in spring; remove any seedlings that occur where you don't want them

Propagate by division or seed

Pests & diseases trouble-free

These delightful plants have a subtle, cool presence that has made them extremely popular in recent years. The flowers are noteworthy for the bracts that surround the flowerhead and that give them their distinctive appearance. Established plants form drifts without becoming invasive.

The flowers, which appear in early to midsummer, are in shades of green through greenish-pinks to reds. The plants offered for sale are all forms of either *Astrantia major* or, less often, of *A. involucrata*. They will grow in sun but are valuable for growing in light shade, where they will make clumps about 60–90 cm (2–3 ft) high and 45 cm (18 in) across. They make good cut flowers.

in the pink

Astrantia maxima is similar to the other astrantias in many ways, but the bracts that surround the flowerheads in early and midsummer are a lovely shell pink, which turns this into a gem of a plant. It will grow in the same positions as its larger cousins and also makes a good cut flower.

Astrantia major

Bergenia Elephant's Ears

Key features excellent groundcover * large, glossy foliage * spikes of bright flowers in spring

Plant in sun or light shade in damp soil, although it will tolerate drier conditions

Care remove dead leaves in spring and then feed and mulch

Propagate by division or from root cuttings

Pests & diseases trouble-free

The common name, elephant's ears, is appropriate for this excellent foliage plant, which has large, leathery, evergreen leaves. They are useful plants because they will tolerate most conditions, growing in sun or shade in moist or dry soil. They are clump-forming and can be used for groundcover.

There is a large number of cultivars to chose from, but there is not a great deal of difference between them. Some have leaves that turn a livery purple in winter, and the flowers, borne in spring, may be white or in shades of pink to reddish-purple. All grow to 30–45 cm (12–18 in) high and about 60 cm (2 ft) across.

hairy leaves

Most bergenias have glossy foliage, but the leaves of *B. ciliata* are covered with short, stiff hairs, which gives the plants a quite different appearance from the most widely grown cultivars. This species is slightly smaller, at about 30–45 cm (12–18 in), and has pale pink flowers and an altogether quieter presence that makes it liked by connoisseurs.

Bergenia cultivar

Brunnera Brunnera

Key features invaluable shade plants * good foliage * hardy

Plant in light shade in most soils, preferably a humus-rich one

Care feed and mulch in spring

Propagate by division or from seed

Pests & diseases trouble-free

These are not startling plants, but they have a wonderful cool presence that shines out in spring, especially if planted in light shade. The species *Brunnera macrophylla* forms clumps with airy sprays of tiny blue or white forget-me-not-like flowers in mid- to late spring.

Brunneras look good in a woodland setting, which in most gardens means under deciduous shrubs. They grow to about 30–45 cm (12–18 in) high and the same across, and although they self-seed gently around, they are not a nuisance, and unwanted seedlings can be easily removed.

silver leaves

The main difference among the various cultivars is the marking on the foliage. Some, such as 'Jack Frost', have almost silver leaves, whereas others, such as 'Langtrees', have spots of silver. The leaves of 'Hadspen Cream' have irregularly shaped ivory margins.

Brunnera macrophylla

Caltha Kingcup, Marsh Marigold

Key features spectacular bright flowers * hardy * needs little attention

Plant in damp soil in sun or light shade

Care water well; mulch if in drier soil

Propagate by division after flowering

Pests & diseases trouble-free

One of the glories of the spring garden is undoubtedly the marsh marigold or kingcup, *Caltha palustris*. The large, buttercup-shaped flowers show up golden, whatever the weather, illuminating their surroundings. They flower quite early in spring and continue for several weeks.

As their name suggests, these are plants for boggy areas, such as beside a pond or stream, although they can be grown in a border that does not dry out too much. They are rather sprawling plants, to 75 cm (30 in) across, and grow to 45 cm (18 in) high. If possible, buy them when they are in bloom because some forms have smaller flowers than others.

go for double

There is a double-flowered form, *C. palustris* 'Flore Pleno', which is really spectacular, brightening the spring garden like nothing else. Like those of the species, the individual flowers are to 4 cm (1½ in) across, carried above dark green leaves.

Caltha palustris 'Flore Pleno'

Campanula Bellflower

Key features bell-shaped flowers ∗ quiet but attractive presence ∗ hardy ∗ reliable

Plant in sun in free-draining soil, although they will grow in heavier ground

Care feed and mulch in spring; cut down in autumn

Propagate by division in spring

Pests & diseases slugs may eat young shoots; otherwise trouble-free

Although they are rarely the showiest of flowers, campanulas are among the treasures of the garden. They have a quiet simplicity that makes them one of the most valued plants in the border. They come in all shapes and sizes, from ground-hugging mats to tall spires.

One of the best is the milky bellflower, *Campanula lactiflora*, of which there are several cultivars. It is a clump-forming plant, to 60 cm (2 ft) across, with tall stems of flowers reaching to 1.2 m (4 ft) or more. The flowers are mainly shades of blue, but there are also white and pink forms.

carpets

Even the smallest garden will have space for *C. poscharskyana*, a carpeting campanula. It is superb for filling those odd, dry corners that you don't know what to do with, and it will also climb walls and through shrubs. The star-like blue flowers are borne from summer until autumn.

Campanula lactiflora

Centaurea Knapweed

Key features interesting flowers ∗ silver-grey foliage ∗ hardy

Plant in any soil, preferably in sun although it will grow in some light shade

Care feed and mulch in spring; cut back after flowering

Propagate by division in spring

Pests & diseases mildew after flowering, but this can be ignored

The knapweeds are interesting plants, which belong to the thistle family although they lack the bad habits of that tribe. The various species and cultivars have a wide range of colours between them and are useful in all situations.

Centaurea montana, 45–60 cm (18–24 in), flowers from late spring to early summer, bearing large, violet-blue flowerheads. The radiating petals have a wonderful airy feel about them. There is also a lovely white form, 'Alba'. They will grow in most soils, their only drawback is that they can sprawl unless supported.

summer alternative

If you have space you could include one of the excellent midsummer forms, such as *Centaurea hypoleuca* 'John Coutts'. This has bright reddish-purple flowers borne over pale green foliage. It slowly makes a large clump and is an excellent border plant.

Centaurea montana

Centranthus Valerian

Key features bright and cheerful * good for gravel beds * hardy

Plant in full sun in well-drained soil, although will grow in heavier soils

Care can self-sow, so remove seedheads early

Propagate from seed sown in autumn or spring

Pests & diseases trouble-free

A visit to the seashore will give a sighting of wild forms of this spectacular plant. It has fleshy, grey-green stems and foliage above which are heads of flowers in various shades of pinks and reds. Red valerian, *Centranthus ruber*, flowers in summer, but if cut back will often reflower in autumn.

This is an excellent choice for a dry or gravel bed, to which it will add vibrant colour. If you can, buy it in flower so that you can get a good red form — some plants have paler, rather pink flowers. They grow to 60 cm (2 ft) or more, but can flop and may need support in exposed places.

contrasting white

The white flowers of *C. ruber* 'Albus' are borne, like those of the species, in dense clusters. They are a lovely foil to the greyish stems and foliage. This is a good candidate for inclusion in a white border, but, like the species, may need staking if it is in an exposed position.

Centranthus ruber

Convallaria Lily-of-the-valley

Key features wonderful scent * attractive appearance * good cut flowers * hardy

Plant in any soil in light shade

Care dig round the edges of the clump each year to stop it from spreading

Propagate by division after flowering

Pests & diseases trouble-free, although flower arrangers can denude your plants

Who can resist this wonderful plant? The dainty spike of pure white bells, held between two dark green leaves, is like a ready-made posy, and the lovely scent is instantly recognizable.

Convallaria majalis flowers from spring to early summer. It will grow in partial shade and prefers reliably moist soil. Its one drawback is that if it is happy it can become a bit invasive. If this happens, simply dig round the edges of the clump to stop it from spreading. Plants are only 15 cm (6 in) high and die back below ground soon after flowering.

seeing pink

Although most people think of the lily-of-the-valley as being white, there is a variety, *rosea*, which has pretty, soft pink flowers. The leaves of the cultivar 'Albostriata' have pale cream stripes, while 'Flore Pleno' bears double white flowers.

Convallaria majalis

Coreopsis Tickseed

Key features attractive flowers and foliage ∗ hardy ∗ good for cutting

Plant in full sun in any reasonable soil

Care feed and mulch in spring; divide and replant if centre of clump begins to die out

Propagate by division in spring

Pests & diseases slugs when the shoots first appear

The daisy family is the source of many fine garden plants, including this one, *Coreopsis verticillata*. For a long period from early summer golden-yellow flowers float above clear green foliage that is so finely divided that it has a filigree effect.

Individual plants grow to 60 cm (24 in) tall and eventually form a spreading, but non-invasive clump about 45 cm (18 in) across. It is an ideal plant for the middle of a border, looking particularly attractive in a hot-coloured border. Slugs enjoy the young shoots when they first appear through the soil, so take preventive action.

pale moonlight

If you prefer something a little subtler, there is a paler form, *C. verticillata* 'Moonbeam', which is identical to the species except that it has paler yellow flowers, which would fit in perfectly with a pastel-coloured scheme.

Coreopsis verticillata

Crambe Crambe

Key features magnificent airy flower display * scented * seedpods good for dried arrangement * hardy

Plant in full sun in any reasonable soil

Care feed and mulch in spring

Propagate by division or from root cuttings

Pests & diseases slugs when the shoots first appear

What a spectacular plant *Crambe cordifolia* can be in early to midsummer! When in flower it reaches 2 m (6 ft) or more tall. The height is provided by clouds of small white flowers, which hover like small butterflies or stars in the air as if they were not supported by anything. To add to this they have a most seductive honey-like perfume.

These are plants for a well-drained position, although they will tolerate heavier soils. Once the flowers fade they are replaced by small seedheads, which are also attractive. They make good dried flowers, but the sprays are often too large to carry indoors.

sea kale

The much smaller species, *Crambe maritima* is known as sea kale, and the common name gives a clue to its preferred habit of pebbly beaches. It produces the same scented flowers as *C. cordifolia* but on a smaller scale. The foliage is an attractive blue-grey.

Crambe cordifolia

Cynara Cardoon

Key features impressive stature * excellent silver foliage * beautiful flowers * can be dried * hardy

Plant in full sun in any reasonable soil

Care feed and mulch in spring

Propagate by division in spring

Pests & diseases trouble-free

Every border needs at least one eye-catching plant to act as a focal point, and *Cynara cardunculus*, the cardoon, is one such plant. It is a magnificent plant, making a vast fountain of silver foliage, and once it has been topped by the huge, purple, thistle-like flowers it is 2.1–2.4 m (7–8 ft) high. Eye-catching indeed.

The individual leaves are large, jaggedly cut but not prickly. The massive purple flowers appear in late summer and are much loved by bumble bees. It is not a difficult plant to grow but it will take a few years to get to full size.

edible and beautiful

You can eat the blanched stems of the cardoon, but it is its relative *C. scolymus*, the globe artichoke, that is more commonly eaten. As well as being a useful vegetable, this can make an excellent border plant, similar to the cardoon but on a smaller scale.

Cynara cardunculus

Delphinium Delphinium

Key features intense blue colours * vertical emphasis to border * hardy

Plant in a sunny position out of the wind in any reasonable soil

Care feed and mulch in spring; support taller plants with canes

Propagate from cuttings or seed

Pests & diseases slugs when the shoots first appear

In the popular image of a cottage garden, delphiniums always have a place, their tall spires of intense blue flowers conjuring up tranquil thoughts of gardens of yesteryear. These lovely plants are, however, still with us, and there are more colours than ever.

As well as bright violet-blue, there is a range of other blues, ranging from the deep blue of 'Faust' to the sky blue of plants in the Summer Skies Group. The cultivar 'Butterball' has lovely cream flowers, and 'Gillian Dallas' has lilac-blue blooms.

Most delphiniums can be grown in an ordinary border with great success. Some grow to 2 m (6 ft) tall and need staking, although many are shorter than this.

shorter forms

As well as the tall delphiniums, there are plenty of smaller plants, which instead of having tall spires of flowers have airy sprays. One such is the beautiful *D. grandiflorum*, 50–60 cm (20–24 in) tall, with dark blue, butterfly-like flowers. This is a lovely plant for a smaller border.

Delphinium cultivar

Dianthus Pink

Key features attractive silver-grey foliage ∗ fragrance ∗ good cut flowers ∗ hardy

Plant in full sun in well-drained soil; they will grow on heavier soils but need replacing more frequently

Care feed in early spring; cut off old flower stems after blooming

Propagate from cuttings in summer

Pests & diseases trouble-free

If you want an informal look to your garden there is nothing better than to have some pinks spilling out over the path. To be a true pink, the plant should have scent as well as a good appearance, and sadly, many modern cultivars lack this essential attribute.

One that does have a lovely scent is 'Doris', which has double pink flowers with a salmon-pink eye, which last well when cut. 'Doris' is easy to grow and is repeat flowering, producing scented blooms from early summer until well into the autumn. It has attractive grey-green foliage and grows to about 30 cm (12 in) tall.

old-fashioned pinks

The old-fashioned pinks are in many ways better than their modern equivalents, but they have the disadvantage that they flower only once, in early summer. However, they are often beautifully scented, which more than compensates. The colours and patterns are also more subtle and satisfying than the more brightly coloured modern ones.

Dianthus cultivar

Diascia Diascia

Key features plentiful flowers
* long season * easy to grow

Plant in sun in reasonably
well-drained soil; they will
grow in heavier soils but are
not so long lived

Care feed in spring; cut back
any long stems in late summer

Propagate from cuttings at
any time

Pests & diseases trouble-free

Diascias are quiet, rather understated plants,
but they are a valuable addition to any
border. The often straggly stems carry small
pink or red flowers over the whole of the
summer and into the autumn.

One of the best of the group, at 30–60 cm (12–24 in),
is *Diascia vigilis*, which is more upright and neater than
many diascias, especially in the form 'Jack Elliott', which
has soft pink flowers and stems that rise to about
30 cm (12 in) or more if it scrambles through a bush.

The plant's long flowering period does mean that the
stems sometimes get a bit long, and they benefit from
being cut back by the end of summer to be replaced by
fresh growth.

red alternative

A lower plant that is suitable for mass planting
at the front of a border is *Diascia barbarae*
'Ruby Field', which has reddish-pink flowers.
It has the same long flowering period, as do
many of the salmon and apricot cultivars, such
as 'Blackthorn Apricot'.

Diascia vigilis 'Jack Elliott'

Dicentra Bleeding Heart

Key features uniquely shaped flowers * graceful stems * good foliage * hardy

Plant in light shade in humus-rich soil

Care feed in early spring; remove plants from the edge of clumps of *D. formosa* and cultivars if they get too big

Propagate by division or from seed in spring

Pests & diseases trouble-free

Many gardeners find the quaint flowers of these plants extremely appealing. The flowers are like lockets or hearts with a tear-drop on each side, and they hang down from one side of the arching stems above the ferny foliage.

The most spectacular form is *Dicentra spectabilis*, which bears flowers in spring on plants that grow to 60 cm (2 ft) or more tall. The long, curved stems of bright pink and white hanging flowers are a lovely contrast with the light green foliage. There is also a wonderful white form, *D. spectabilis* 'Alba', although it is not as robust as the species and needs a shady corner where it will not be overgrown by thuggish neighbours.

silver foliage

There is a group of cultivars that goes under the general name of *D. formosa* that is well worth growing. These are about 45–60 cm (18–24 in) and have finely cut, silvery leaves, above which are stems of red-pink or pearly white flowers in spring and early summer. They quickly form large clumps.

Dicentra spectabilis

Doronicum Leopard's Bane

Key features bright flowers that stand out ∗ easy to grow ∗ spring flowering ∗ hardy

Plant in light shade or sun in any reasonable garden soil

Care feed and mulch in early spring; cut back any plants spreading out too far

Propagate by division after flowering

Pests & diseases trouble-free

There are few plants better than leopard's bane for brightening up the spring and early summer garden. The flowers are a wonderful golden-yellow and are beautifully displayed against the light green foliage. The petals of the daisy-like flowers radiate from a central disc of the same colour.

There are several species, but they resemble each other so closely that they have become rather mixed up. The larger ones grow to 1 m (3 ft) tall, but most are a bit shorter than this. They form a carpet and over the years can become a little invasive, but they are easy to control by simply cutting them back.

little leo

There is one excellent form for the small garden: 'Little Leo' grows to only about 25 cm (10 in) high, but it carries the same large, golden-yellow, daisy-like flowers as the larger forms. Another cultivar well worth looking out for is 'Finesse', which has narrow, elegant petals and grows to about 50 cm (25 in) tall.

Doronicum orientale

Echinacea Echinacea

Key features colourful flowers
* strong plants * good cut
flowers * hardy

Plant in sun in any reasonable
garden soil

Care feed and mulch in spring

Propagate by division for
named clones or from seed for
species

Pests & diseases trouble-free

Echinacea has recently become well known for its medicinal properties, but it has long been valued as a garden plant. *Echinacea purpurea* is another member of the large and valuable daisy family. The flowers have purple petals and a reddish-gold central boss. They are large, up to 15 cm (6 in) or more across, and appear over a long period in summer.

This is a clump-forming plant, with sturdy stems that need no support except in really exposed gardens. The stems reach up 1.2 m (4 ft), making it a good plant for the middle or back of the border. The flower stems can also be cut and used in flower arrangements.

white alternative

As well as the purple-flowered form, there are also greenish-white ones, but still with the reddish-yellow central disc. Although the flowers are not true white, they are nevertheless attractive. 'White Swan', is one of the best cultivars, the plants grow to 60 cm (24 cm) tall.

Echinacea purpurea

Echinops Globe Thistle

Key features strong, upright plants * unusual and attractive flowers * attractive to bees * good cut flowers * hardy

Plant in full sun in any reasonable garden soil

Care feed and mulch in spring; cut down after flowering

Propagate by division or from root cuttings

Pests & diseases trouble-free

There is nothing quite like the globe thistle. These plants produce perfectly spherical flowerheads, which are borne in late summer on erect stems above the dark green leaves.

The form usually grown is *Echinops ritro*, most often in the old cultivar 'Veitch's Blue', which has dark blue flowers, loved by bees. The disappointment is that the foliage is nothing special. In spite of its silvery colour, it has a ragged appearance and often hangs limply. The plant's height, 1–1.2 m (3–4 ft), means, however, that it is usually grown in the middle of the border, where the leaves are hidden by other plants. Don't let this aspect of the plant put you off trying it.

towering white

E. sphaerocephalum is quite different. It has greener leaves, which are no less untidy, but has striking white globes of flowers, each to 6 cm (2½ in) across. It is taller, to 2 m (6 ft) high, making it a valuable back-of-the-border plant, where, again, the foliage is hidden. Remove the flowerheads as they go over if you do not want self-sown seedlings to appear.

Echinops ritro

Epimedium Barrenwort

Key features excellent for shady areas * good groundcover * unusual but beautiful flowers * good tinted foliage

Plant in light shade or full sun in any reasonable garden soil

Care cut down to ground in midwinter and feed and mulch at the same time

Propagate by division after flowering

Pests & diseases trouble-free

There are few really first-class plants for shady positions, but this is one of them. It forms a dense mass of attractive foliage, which suppresses weeds and, in early spring, produces flowers in red, yellow or purple. The flowers are like jester's hats, hanging from arching stems and swaying in the breeze.

Epimedium grandiflorum is one of the best, particularly in the form 'Rose Queen', which has pink flowers. To get the best out of the plants cut them to the ground in midwinter so that the new young growth shoots in spring when the flowers appear. Plants are only 20–30 cm (8–12 in) high but spread to 30 cm (12 in) or more.

tiny delights

There is an increasing number of dwarf cultivars, all of which are eminently worth growing. The lovely 'Nanum', to 8 cm (3 in) tall, has white flowers, and 'Lilafee', which grows to 23 cm (9 in) tall, has pretty purple flowers and purplish-green foliage.

Epimedium x *youngianum* 'Niveum'

Erigeron Mexican daisy

Key features attractive, airy flowers * long flowering season * hardy

Plant in sun in any soil

Care cut back the entire plant in early spring to where new growth is forming

Propagate from seed or self-sown seedlings

Pests & diseases trouble-free

Of all the perennial daisies this is the one that bears flowers most closely resembling the common daisy that grows in our lawns. *Erigeron karvinskianus*, however, is a clump-forming plant, covered with white and pink, yellow-centred flowers that are carried on slender stems over a long period from spring until winter.

It grows to about 30 cm (12 in) high, and although it can be grown as a front-of-border plant, it is an excellent choice for growing in the cracks of paving or steps. Once established, it sows itself around, often finding the perfect place for itself.

larger flowers

Not all erigerons have the dainty flowers of *E. karvinskianus*. Cultivars such as 'Dimity' (pink), 'Dunkelste Aller' (dark purple) and 'Schneewitchen' (white) have much larger flowers, to 5 cm (2 in) across, but they also flower over a long period and, at about 25 cm (10 in) high, are good front-of-border plants.

Erigeron karvinskianus

Eryngium Sea holly

Key features eye-catching ∗ good colours ∗ good foliage ∗ excellent for cutting and drying

Plant in full sun ideally in free-draining soil, but will tolerate most conditions

Care feed in spring; cut to the ground in winter

Propagate by division or from root cuttings

Pests & diseases trouble-free

It's worth finding space for at least one representative of this distinctive and wonderful group of plants in a perennial garden. They are characterized by stiff, prickly foliage, often silver or blue in colour, and flowerheads that are surrounded by stiff bracts and domed heads.

One of the best is *Eryngium* x *oliverianum*, which grows to 60–75 cm (24–30 in) tall and bears large heads of beautiful, steely blue flowers from midsummer to early autumn. The stems and leaves are also steely blue, and they make ideal plants for the flower arranger, either fresh or dried. Take care when you are weeding around the prickly foliage.

haze of heads

Eryngium x *tripartitum* is a bushier plant, 60–90 x 50 cm (24–36 x 20 in), which produces a haze of branches bearing many tiny blue flowers. In contrast *E. yuccifolium* is a tall plant, about 1.2 m (4 ft) high, producing single stems with a clustered flowerhead at the top and spiny, strap-like leaves at the base.

Eryngium x *tripartitum*

Eupatorium Joe Pye weed

Key features imposing ∗
attracts bees ∗ late-flowering ∗
haze of colour ∗ hardy

Plant in sun in any soil,
including heavy ones

Care feed and mulch in spring

Propagate by division in
spring

Pests & diseases slugs can
eat the young shoots

These rather coarse plants make magnificent displays for the back of a border, where the flowers will be adored by bees and butterflies. *Eupatorium purpureum* is the biggest of the group, with purple stems reaching 2–2.4 m (6–8 ft) high. From late summer to early autumn they are topped with pinkish-purple flowers.

These imposing plants need a lot of space and are not suitable for small gardens, although there are some shorter cultivars, including *E. maculatum* 'Atropureum', which has bright pink flowers. Eupatoriums do spread, although not invasively, and they may need cutting back from time to time. To keep these plants going at their best it is important to feed them regularly.

smaller whites

There are several other species in the genus that, although not as imposing as *E. purpureum,* are still fine plants. White snakeroot, *E. rugosum,* for example, has small white flowers on 1 m (3 ft) stems and is suited to a smaller garden.

Eupatorium purpureum

Euphorbia Spurge, Milkweed

Key features irritant sap ★ beautiful flowerheads ★ good for focal points ★ hardy

Plant ideally in sun in free-draining soil, although they will grow in partial shade and heavier soils

Care feed in spring and cut out any dead stems, being careful of the sap

Propagate from seed sown in spring

Pests & diseases trouble-free

There are thousands of spurges, and although not all are suitable for gardens, a lot of them are. One of the best is *Euphorbia characias* subsp. *wulfenii*, which forms large clumps of tall stems topped with heads of yellow flowers surrounded by green bracts.

These eye-catching plants, to 1.2 m (4 ft) high and across, make good focal points and can be used at key points. Once established, leave the plants in place because they are difficult to move. All euphorbias exude a white latex sap when the stems are cut or damaged. This can cause skin irritation, and it is excruciatingly painful if you get any sap in your eyes. Although it would be a shame not to grow these beautiful plants, if you feel worried about them, don't.

prostrate but pretty

Not all euphorbias are large. The evergreen *E. myrsinites* has blue-green leaves, arranged spirally around prostrate stems. In spring long-lasting, bright yellow flowerheads are borne on the ends of the stems. Plants grow to only about 10 cm (4 in) tall and spread to 30 cm (12 in).

Euphorbia griffithii

Filipendula Meadowsweet

Key features colourful * tidy clumps * good foliage * hardy

Plant in sun in damp soil or any reasonable garden soil

Care feed and mulch in spring; cut down in autumn or winter

Propagate by division in spring

Pests & diseases trouble-free

These attractive plants are one of the mainstays of a wildlife or bog garden, producing wonderful drifts of pink, white or red blooms in summer. The tiny flowers are carried in clusters that are held well above the pleated leaves, which can be purplish in colour. Plants grow to 1–1.2 m (3–4 ft) high and are good for the middle or back of a border.

Filipendula palmata is one of the best species. It forms a spreading clump without becoming invasive and bears pale to deep pink flowers in midsummer. It does particularly well in damp soil, but will, in fact, grow in any reasonable garden soil.

other choices

There are several other species that are worth growing, including *Filipendula purpurea* and *F. rubra*. There is not a great deal of difference between them, and one is usually enough in a small garden. The white-flowered meadowsweet, *F. ulmaria*, is known for its strong, sweet scent.

Filipendula rubra 'Venusta'

Foeniculum Fennel

Key features elegant *
beautiful foliage * leaves can
be used in cooking * hardy

Plant in sun in any soil, even
poor ones

Care remove flowerheads
before the seed is set to
prevent unwanted seedlings

Propagate from seed sown
in spring

Pests & diseases trouble-free

Fennel is a wonderful plant for the border,
especially in its bronze-leaved form,
Foeniculum vulgare 'Purpureum'. The foliage
is extremely finely cut and feathery and, in
spite of the name 'Purpureum', has a distinct
bronze colour. It is a tall plant, the flat heads
of yellow flowers swaying 2 m (6 ft) or more
above the ground in mid- to late summer.

The leaves are diaphanous, so although this is a tall
plant it can be situated almost anywhere in the border,
including the front, because you can see through it. It
self-seeds prolifically, so if you do not want the dozens
of seedlings that will appear cut off the seedheads
before they are shed.

big boy

Although belonging to a different genus *Ferula
communis* is closely related and is in fact a giant
fennel. The foliage is superb and very finely
dissected. It is green rather than bronze but that
is of little matter with such a beautiful plant. It
grows to over 2 m (7 ft) and is an eye-catcher.

Foeniculum vulgare

Galega Goat's rue

Key features soft blue or white flowers * robust plant * hardy

Plant in full sun in any reasonable soil

Care feed and mulch in spring; deadhead to prevent seeding

Propagate from seed or by division in spring

Pests & diseases trouble-free

The back of the border is an important area although sometimes difficult to plant, and colourful plants that can peep over their neighbours are most welcome.

Galega officinalis is one such. It bears clusters of lavender-blue or white, pea-like flowers from early summer to early autumn. The white flowers of *G. officinalis* 'Alba' in particular show up beautifully against a dark green hedge, such as yew.

Galegas have taproots and cannot be moved easily, so it is important to get the position right the first time. Although the species grows to 1.5 m (5 ft) or more high, it rarely needs support. It does not spread, but it can seed around, so deadhead before the seed is set, unless you want to collect it for sowing.

brighter blue

The species *Galega orientalis* is similar in many ways to its larger relative but it grows to about 1.2 m (4 ft) high and to 60 cm (2 ft) across. In late spring to early summer it bears racemes of attractive deep purple-blue flowers. Unfortunately, this species has the habit of sending out underground rhizomes, and it can be invasive.

Galega x hartlandii 'Alba'

Gaura Gaura

Key features airy butterfly flowers * goes well with other plants * hardy

Plant in full sun, preferably in well-drained soil but it will just tolerate heavier ground

Care cut back in autumn; feed and mulch in spring

Propagate from basal cuttings and seed in spring

Pests & diseases trouble-free

This increasingly popular plant has white or pink flowers that are carried on airy stems so that they appear to be suspended like dancing butterflies.

The species *Gaura lindheimeri* bears large clusters of pinkish-white flowers from late spring to early summer. It grows to about 1.5 m (5 ft) tall and is a rather floppy plant, so is best grown among other plants that will not only support it but also complement its flowers. Grasses are a popular accompaniment, and the smoky foliage of bronze fennel is also excellent. Because gauras have taproots established plants should not be moved.

in the pink

The species is tougher and longer lasting than some of its cultivars. 'Siskiyou Pink', for example, which many gardeners prefer to the species, is not the strongest of plants, but the flowers, which are strongly marked with deep pink, are very pretty. 'Corrie's Gold' has gold-variegated foliage.

Gaura lindheimeri

Geranium Cranesbill

The Cranesbills provide one of the largest ranges of garden plants and the hundreds of species and varieties are useful for nearly all gardens. The best are those that flower for most of the summer, for example *Geranium* 'Patricia', while others, such as *Geranium magnificum*, have a short but glorious season.

Geraniums are very easy to cultivate and need little attention. Most of the shorter season forms can be cut to the ground after flowering when they will produce a fresh crop of leaves making them valuable foliage plants for the rest of the season. There are forms that vary in height from only a few centimetres to 1 m (4–36 in). Use where you need a splash of colour.

Key features colourful * reliable * easy to look after * hardy

Plant most prefer sun, but there are also plenty for shady areas

Care feed and mulch in spring; remove spent flowerheads

Propagate most by division or from basal cuttings in spring; species from seed

Pests & diseases generally trouble-free, but vine weevils can be a nuisance for some; hand-pick grubs and adults and kill them

upfront

One of the best for front of border situations is *Geranium sanguineum* and its many varieties. These provide a long season of many purple flowers although there are also pink and white cultivars. They vary in size from ground-hugging to about 30 cm (12 in).

Geranium x *magnificum*

Geum Geum, Avens

Key features fresh-looking *
long flowering season * good
front-of-border plants * hardy

Plant in sun in any reasonable
garden soil

Care remove the flowerheads
once flowering is over; feed
and mulch in spring

Propagate by division in
spring

Pests & diseases trouble-free

Geums can be divided into two broad groups.
One group, largely derived from *Geum rivale*,
have nodding, almost bell-like flowers; the
other, developed mainly from *G. chiloense*
and *G. coccineum*, have bright discs that look
you in the eye.

Plants form small clumps that bear their flowers in
early summer and sometimes have a smaller, second
flowering towards autumn. The flowers are either
shades of pink or yellow. The old cultivar *G. rivale*
'Leonard's Variety', to 45 cm (18 in) tall, is still one of
the best, with its soft pink flowers, blushed with red
and apricot. These are well-behaved plants with no
tendency to become invasive.

cheerful chappy

The group with flat, broader flowers include
some wonderful garden plants. Some, such as
G. 'Borisii', 30–50 x 30–45 cm (12–20 x
12–18 in), have really bright flowers, in this
case orange-red, which cheer up even the
dullest of days. They make good foliage plants
when not in flower.

Geum rivale 'Leonard's Variety'

Gunnera Gunnera

Key features enormous *
impressive * for larger gardens
only * foliage plant

Plant in sun in damp soil next
to a pond

Care cover the crowns with
the dying leaves in autumn to
protect it from frosts; feed and
mulch in spring

Propagate by division

Pests & diseases trouble-free

And now for something big, really big!
Gunnera manicata is grown for its foliage,
the individual roundish leaves of which can
be 2 m (6 ft) or more across. It is possible
to shelter under them when it is raining,
but take care that you do not rub against
the stiff bristles.

These giant plants, which eventually grow to 2.4 m
(8 ft) tall and 4 m (12 ft) or more across, are obviously
for larger gardens and are normally grown beside
water, where they make a wonderful feature. The
flowerheads are also enormous – to 1 m (3 ft) or more
– but, surprisingly, are not conspicuous being a dull
green. It is easy to grow and widely available.

something smaller

There are some species that are completely at the
other end of the scale and are only a couple of
centimetres (1 in) high, but they are tender. On
the other hand there is *Gunnera tinctoria* which is
like the above but on a smaller scale, much better
suited to the smaller garden.

Gunnera manicata

Helenium Sneezeweed, Helen's flower

Key features colourful ★ self-supporting ★ long flowering season ★ hardy

Plant in sun in any reasonable garden soil, including quite heavy ground

Care feed and mulch in spring

Propagate by division in spring

Pests & diseases slugs in early spring when growth first appears

Herbaceous borders could have been specially created for heleniums. They are tall, upright plants that spread slowly to form a clump, and when they are grown in a drift they give colour to the border over a long period in summer, sometimes into autumn.

The daisy-like flowers are in shades of brown, orange, yellow and red. One of the best cultivars is *Helenium* 'Moerheim Beauty', which has petals of an underlying warm gold colour generously splashed with red and brown radiating from a dark brown central boss. These are carried on stems 1.2 m (4 ft) or more long, which generally do not need supporting. This is a wonderful plant for hot-coloured borders.

all yellow

There are some cultivars that are a single colour. *Helenium* 'Butterpat', for example, has butter-yellow petals and a slightly deeper golden-yellow central disc. These look great growing in a pastel-coloured border.

Helenium 'Ragamuffin'

Helleborus Hellebore

Key features winter flowering
* graceful * wide range of
colours * hardy

Plant in light shade in any
reasonable garden soil

Care cut off the old leaves at
the beginning of the year; feed
and mulch at the same time

Propagate by division in late
spring or from seed sown
fresh

Pests & diseases cut off any
foliage suffering from
blackspot

In recent years hellebores have become
increasingly widely grown, largely because
their nodding flowers provide colour and
interest in winter and early spring when little
else is in bloom in the garden.

The various varieties that catch most people's attention
have been lumped under the general name *Helleborus
x hybridus*. The flowers are shallow dishes, which
in the majority of cases unfortunately look at the
ground. The colours vary from bright green through
white to yellow, pinks, purples to slatey blacks. There
are now some rather beautiful doubles becoming
available. They are perfect plants to fill odd spots in
shady parts of the garden.

think species

While most gardeners concentrate on the
hybrids, the connoisseurs are turning to the
species of which many are very beautiful in
their simplicity of form and colour. Take a
look at plants such as *Helleborus torquatus*
or *H. dumetorum*.

Helleborus x hybridus

Hemerocallis Daylily

Key features colourful ∗ good foliage ∗ wide choice of colours ∗ hardy

Plant in sun or light shade in any reasonable garden soil

Care feed and mulch in spring; lift and divide in spring if clumps become congested

Propagate by division in spring

Pests & diseases trouble-free

All herbaceous borders should contain at least one daylily. They form large fountains of strap-like leaves from which arise leafless stems carrying lily-like, trumpet-shaped flowers. These open in the morning and fade in the evening, hence the common name, to be replaced by another flower the next day.

The hybrids flower at different times throughout the summer, so it is possible to have a long season of colour. There are several thousand cultivars to choose from in a wide range of colours, blue being the only one missing from the palette. They grow up to 1.2 m (4 ft) high but are not invasive plants. If, after a number of years, the clumps become congested simply lift, divide and replant some of the divisions.

early birds

Some daylilies flower early in the season. 'Corky' (yellow with brown-backed petals) and 'Golden Chimes' (golden-yellow with maroon-backed petals) bloom in early summer. The species _Hemerocallis lilioasphodelus_, one of the first to flower, is also worth seeking out.

Hemerocallis 'Lusty Lealand'

Heuchera Heuchera, Coral flower

Key features attractive foliage * airy flowers * front-of-border plant * hardy

Plant in sun or light shade in any good garden soil

Care feed and mulch

Propagate by division in spring

Pests & diseases vine weevils can be a problem; remove all soil from newly purchased plants and replace with clean soil; hand pick and kill any adults or grubs you find

Heucheras have become popular in recent years, as much for their foliage as for their flowers. The pretty flowers are like tiny bells, suspended from thin, leafless stems that rise to a height of about 45 cm (18 in) above the mounds of foliage.

The foliage is mainly valued for its markings and coloration, and although there are plenty of new cultivars to choose from, one of the best is still *Heuchera villosa* 'Palace Purple', which has dark bronze-red foliage above which, in midsummer, are borne greenish-cream flowers. Although heucheras will grow in shade, the best coloration is generally seen on plants grown in full sun.

dancing fairies

One of the best of the new introductions, giving a long season of interest, is *Heuchera* 'Ebony and Ivory', which has excellent dark brown foliage, above which fly tiny white flowers. It will grow in either partial shade or sun, and the flowers rise to 45 cm (18 in) high.

Heuchera micrantha var. *diversifolia* 'Palace Purple'

Hosta Hosta

Key features excellent groundcover * wonderful foliage * graceful flowers * hardy

Plant in sun or shade and in any reasonable garden soil

Care feed and mulch in early spring

Propagate by division in spring

Pests & diseases slugs love hostas

Hostas are one of the backbone plants for the herbaceous garden. Their clumps or carpets of leaves act as a foil to more colourful plants in the border, and they can be grown in either sun or shade or in containers.

Hostas are grown for their varied foliage shapes, colours, ranging from almost blue to bright emerald green and yellow-green, and textures, from smooth and glossy to crinkled. There are also many variegated varieties, of which *Hosta fortunei* var. *albopicta*, which has yellow-green leaves irregularly edged with darker green, is one of the most attractive. *H. fortunei* var. *aureomarginata* has dark green leaves edged with yellow-green.

life in miniature

Over the years thousands of cultivars have been developed, most growing to 40–60 x 60–100 cm (16–24 x 24–36 in). However, one of the smallest, 'Thumb Nail', has tiny green leaves that form a carpet only 3 cm (1¼ in) high.

Hosta fortunei var. *albopicta*

Inula Inula

Key features golden flowers over a long period * easy to grow * hardy

Plant in sun in any reasonable soil

Care feed and mulch in spring

Propagate by division or from seed in spring

Pests & diseases trouble-free

This is another example of the enormously useful daisy family. All inulas have yellow petals around darker yellow central discs, and they bloom from midsummer to early autumn, providing bright colours over a long period in mixed borders.

One of the best is *Inula hookeri*, which flowers from late summer to mid-autumn. It has furry foliage and stems rising to 75 cm (30 in). The flowers, which are about 5 cm (2 in) across, have delicate, pale yellow petals, almost like thin gold wire, around brown-yellow discs.

Inulas will grow in most soils, but *I. hookeri* prefers slightly damper conditions. It has a tendency to spread, but it is generally not a nuisance and can be cut back if it extends too far beyond its allotted space.

reach for the sky

Although most inula flowers are similar in shape, size and colour, the size of the plants varies considerably. *I. magnifica* grows to 2.1 m (7 ft) or more and will be an impressive presence at the back of a border.

Inula hookeri

Iris Iris

Key features eye-catching flowers * attractive foliage * good cut flowers * hardy

Plant in full sun in any reasonable soil

Care feed in spring but do not mulch over the rhizomes

Propagate by division after flowering

Pests & diseases slugs can be a nuisance

This is a large genus that contains some of the most familiar garden plants. The distinctive and beautiful flowers are available in a wide range of colours and patterns, and it's possible to find almost every shade and combination of colours.

The bearded irises, sometimes known as flags or Germanic irises, emerge from thick rhizomes that grow near the surface of the soil. They need a sunny position, and you should take care that other plants don't grow between them. Every year new cultivars are developed, and your choice will be determined by the colour wanted. 'Beverley Sills' bears coral pink blooms in early summer. 'Dusky Challenger' has purple flowers with violet beards in late spring to early summer.

Siberian irises

Siberian irises have a quieter, gentler charm than their larger, more brightly coloured cousins. They grow to only about 60 cm (2 ft) tall. The main colours are variations on blue, but white and yellow forms are also available. They prefer moist soil.

Iris bearded cultivar

Kirengeshoma Kirengeshoma

Key features beautiful foliage, stems and flowers * good autumn plant * good for shade * hardy

Plant in light shade in any reasonable soil, although it prefers moisture-retentive, lime-free ground

Care feed and mulch in spring

Propagate by division or from seed in spring

Pests & diseases trouble-free

Kirengeshoma palmata is not a showy plant, and its subtlety is its main charm. It is a woodland plant, but instead of flowering in spring, as most woodland plants do, the flowers appear in late summer and into autumn, providing colour and interest in areas that can be quite dull at this time of year.

It has purplish-black stems, which carry green, palmate leaves that float airily above the soil. Above this are the pale yellow flowers, which are shaped a bit like inverted shuttlecocks. Established plants grow to about 1 m (3 ft) high.

Japanese or Korean

Some plants are available as *K. palmata* Koreana Group. These are very similar to the species but tend to grow taller, to about 2 m (6 ft), and have more open flowers, borne on more erect stems.

Kirengeshoma palmata

Knautia Knautia

Key features useful colour * long season * hardy

Plant in full sun in any reasonable garden soil

Care feed and mulch in spring; keep plants upright by giving some form of support

Propagate by division or from seed in spring

Pests & diseases mildew, but this can be safely ignored

This is a rather sprawling plant, but it makes up for its habit as it has delightful crimson flowers, a relatively uncommon colour in the garden. The pincushion-like flowers are similar to those of scabious (see pages 206–7), to which it is related.

Knautia macedonica is not a particularly neat plant, but it can be improved considerably by supporting it with peasticks or by some other method. When supported, it grows to 60–75 cm (24–30 in) tall and 30–45 cm (12–18 in) across. The foliage is a greyish-green, the greyness provided by the slight covering of downy hairs. The flowers appear over a long period from early summer right through to the first frosts.

pastels

Until recently the only forms of *K. macedonica* that you could get were those with deep crimson flowers, but recently a number of pastel-coloured forms with blooms in shades of pale pink, mauve and purple have become available. These are usually grown from seed.

Knautia macedonica pastel form

Kniphofia Red-hot Poker

Key features bold, dramatic plants ∗ hot colours ∗ self-supporting ∗ hardy

Plant in full sun in any reasonable garden soil

Care remove foliage in early spring; feed and mulch at the same time

Propagate by division in spring

Pests & diseases trouble-free

These plants always stand out in the border, creating an eye-catching focal point. The foliage forms a fountain of narrow leaves, from which arise leafless stems carrying the candle-flame flowers. The colour varies but is usually red or yellow or a combination.

There is a huge range of cultivars, which vary in height, from about 45 cm (18 in) to over 2 m (6 ft), and flowering time, from early summer to mid-autumn. Each plant makes a clump but rarely strays from its allotted space. They are hardy, but it is best to leave the foliage on until early spring to protect the crown from frost. Although tall they do not need staking. Among the best yellow forms is 'Ice Queen', which produces spikes, to 1.2 m (4 ft) tall, of creamy yellow flowers.

green fingers

Among the red-hot pokers are some that have cool-looking flowers. These are almost green, although they still have a hint of yellow. 'Percy's Pride', to 1.2 m (4 ft) tall, has yellow flowers opening from green buds, from late summer to early autumn.

Kniphofia 'Painted Lady'

Lamium Dead Nettle

Key features carpeting * good flowers and good foliage * mixes well with other plants * hardy

Plant in sun in any garden soil

Care cut back as summer progresses to prevent plants getting straggly

Propagate by division in spring

Pests & diseases trouble-free

Dead nettles are grown as groundcover in areas of the garden that can otherwise be difficult to plant, such as in shady corners or under trees, and their attractive leaves and pretty flowers are a welcome addition to the garden.

One of the most attractive is *Lamium maculatum*, particularly in its pink-flowered form 'Roseum', and it is a delightful carpeting plant. It does spread a bit but is easily pulled up if it strays too far. The species grows to 15–20 cm (6–8 in) high. Red-purple, pink or white flowers appear in spring to summer. The almost triangular leaves are green but splashed with silver-white markings, so it is a useful foliage plant when it is not in flower. It can be used by itself at the front of a border or allowed to thread between other plants.

spring dome

Quite a different plant is *L. orvala*, which forms an impressive dome of upright stems to 45–60 cm (18–24 in) high. In spring it produces large, dusky pink flowers hidden among the light green foliage. This will grow well even in light shade.

Lamium maculatum

Lathyrus Flowering Pea

Key features non-climbing *
excellent colours * spring
flowering * hardy

Plant in light shade or sun in
any garden soil

Care remove the seedpods
before they burst if you don't
want extra seedlings

Propagate from seed

Pests & diseases trouble-free

The pea family is a large one, and it is well
represented in our gardens. Many are
climbers, but there are a few earth-bound
species, including the delightful *Lathyrus
vernus*. This forms a small hummock, only
about 30 cm (12 in) high, which is
smothered with red and blue flowers in early
spring. There is also a form 'Alboroseus',
which has soft pink and white flowers.

This is a woodland plant, and although it will grow in
the open it does best grown under deciduous shrubs,
in spaces that would not otherwise be used because
they are covered in foliage later in the year.

large flowers

Another treasure from this genus is the
everlasting pea, *L. grandiflorus*. This is a
scrambler and likes nothing better than to climb
45–60 cm (18–24 in) up through a shrub,
although it will stand on its own in a tangled
clump. The flowers are large and of a strong red
and blue, but unfortunately are not scented.

Lathyrus grandiflorus

Liatris Blazing Star, Kansas Gay Feather

Key features distinct growth habit * colourful * good mid-border plant * hardy

Plant in a sunny position in any reasonable garden soil

Care feed and mulch in spring

Propagate by division for cultivars; species from seed; both in spring

Pests & diseases slugs can be a problem with emerging growth

This unusual, mid-border plant produces bottlebrush-like spikes of flowers. It has the unusual characteristic that the flowers open at the top of the spike first, moving downwards rather than vice versa.

There are several liatris to grow, but one of the most popular is *Liatris spicata*, which has bright mauve-purple flowers in late summer to mid-autumn. The more commonly available form, *L. spicata* 'Kobold', has more pinkish flowers. A white form, 'Alba', is also easy to obtain. The grassy leaves are not particularly interesting, and all grow to around 60 cm (2 ft) tall. They add to the appearance of the border without drawing attention to themselves.

elegance

The quiet presence of *L. spicata* is matched and in some ways superseded by the elegant prairie blazing star, *L. aspera*, which is less well known. The mauve-purple flowers, borne in late summer to early autumn, are spaced more widely on the stem, and plants can grow to 1.2 m (4 ft) tall.

Liatris spicata

Ligularia Ligularia

Key features bold plants ∗ good foliage ∗ golden-yellow flowers ∗ good in damp spots

Plant in sun or light shade in damp or even wet soil

Care feed and mulch in spring

Propagate by division

Pests & diseases slugs adore them

These tall, rather imposing members of the daisy family are suitable for the rougher, wetter parts of the garden, especially near ponds or streams, and they are particularly valuable for adding colour to borders in late summer to early autumn.

Ligularia dentata, 1–1.5 m (3–5 ft) tall, is one of the more refined members of the genus. It is sometimes known as golden groundsel, and it produces large, heart-shaped leaves, each to 30 cm (12 in) long, which are dark green on the upper surface and dark mahogany on the underside. From midsummer to early autumn it bears large clusters of orange-yellow flowers. The cultivars 'Desdemona' and 'Othello' are two of the best, both growing to about 1 m (3 ft) tall. The damp conditions that these plants like also suit the slugs that love the leaves.

yellow rockets

Most ligularias have heads of large orange-yellow daisies, but some, including *L. przewalskii* and the hybrid 'The Rocket', have spikes of delicate bright yellow flowers that look like the trail of sparks behind a rocket.

Ligularia dentata

Limonium Sea lavender, Statice

Key features long flowering season * good cut and dried flower * hardy

Plant in full sun in any reasonable garden soil

Care feed and mulch in spring

Propagate by division or from seed

Pests & diseases trouble-free

Limoniums are good plants for the front of a border. The flowers are borne late in the season, so they are useful for disguising other plants that have started to go over and that look a little untidy.

The leaves of *Limonium platyphyllum* are quite large, leathery and dark green, all coming from the base and forming a rosette. Out of the rosettes rise thin, wiry stems with several branches all carrying tiny lavender-blue flowers along their upper parts, creating a lavender haze above the foliage. Look out for the cultivars 'Robert Butler' and 'Violetta'. They all make good flowers for cutting and can be used fresh or dried. Several planted together make a fine drift of colour for a long period in summer.

perennial annual

L. sinuatum is another perennial statice, but it is not reliably hardy and is usually grown as an annual. It bears dense clusters of tiny, funnel-shaped, pink, white or blue flowers. There are several cultivars that have a wide range of flower colours, including bright yellow, blue and shades of apricot.

Limonium sinuatum

Linaria Toadflax

Key features airy structure *
long season * hardy

Plant in a sunny position in
any garden soil, including
poor ones

Care cut back spent flower
stems before they seed

Propagate from seed in spring

Pests & diseases trouble-free

Linaria purpureum is a widely grown plant,
bearing upright stems of tiny snapdragon-like
flowers in a clear purple. This creates an airy
display up to 60 cm (2 ft) high over a long
period during the summer months.

The narrow leaves are greyish-green and up to 6 cm
(2½ in) long. Plants self-seed, always providing plenty
of spare seedlings, although they are easy enough to
remove if not required. There is a pretty pink cultivar,
'Canon Went', and a white one, 'Springside White', both
of which are worth searching out.

yellow dragon

L. dalmaticum is an altogether bigger plant,
with tall stems of bright yellow, snapdragon-like
flowers. It can grow to 1 m (3 ft) tall and is
useful for adding a splash of colour to the
middle of a border.

Linaria purpureum

Linum Flax

Key features good blue flowers * long season * hardy

Plant in a warm, sunny position and preferably in well-drained soil, although they will tolerate heavier ones

Care cut off flower stems after flowering but collect a few seeds first

Propagate from seed in spring

Pests & diseases trouble-free

If you want blue flowers this may be the plant for you. The leaves are small and of little significance, but the flowers are beautiful. They appear daily on long, thin, arching stems. Each flower is funnel shaped and a wonderful clear blue. After a few days of flowering the ground beneath the plant is also blue, from fallen petals.

Linum perenne and the similar *L. narbonense* are not long-lived plants, but they come readily from seed, so always collect a few before you cut off the old stems. Although each flower is short-lived, there is a continuance of flowers, which gives a long season. Both species grow to 45–60 cm (18–24 in) high.

golden funnels

L. flavum, 15 cm (6 in), is a cheerful plant. It has golden-yellow, funnel-shaped flowers emerging from dark green foliage. The cultivar 'Gemmell's Hybrid' has blue-green leaves and bright yellow flowers. It is only 15 cm (6 in) high, but it looks splendid in the front of a well-drained border.

Linum perenne

Liriope Lilyturf

Key features autumn flowering * blue flowers * hardy

Plant in a sunny position in any reasonable soil

Care feed and mulch in spring; at the same time cut off all foliage

Propagate by division in spring

Pests & diseases trouble-free

This plant can look rather untidy for a large part of the year, but it comes into its own in autumn when it throws up stems of spherical, bright blue flowers. At this time of year this is invaluable because there are not that many blue flowers around.

The leaves of *Liriope muscari* are narrow and strap-like and form a miniature fountain. They can look scruffy on established plants, but if you cut them all off in spring a new set will replace the old. The plants can create a dense clump 30–45 cm (12–18 in), which can become congested and also too large, but it is easy to lift in spring and divide it, replacing just a few of the divisions to start a new clump.

new varieties

There is an increasing number of new cultivars, several of which have variegated foliage. 'John Burch', for example, has golden-variegated leaves and tall flower spikes, and 'Variegata' and 'Gold-banded' have gold-striped leaves. Also worth growing is 'Monroe White', which has white flowers and is ideal for a shady spot.

Liriope muscari

Lupinus Lupin

Key features colourful flowers
* wide range of colours
* scented * hardy

Plant in full sun in any
reasonable garden soil

Care feed and mulch in
spring; remove heads after
flowering

Propagate from cuttings or
seed in spring

Pests & diseases lupin
aphids

Who could fail to love lupins? The tall spires of flowers provide an air of serenity in the garden, and they not only provide colour in the mid- to late summer border but also a wonderful peppery scent.

The plants are quite tall, to 1.2 m (4 ft) high, and when the flowers are over cut them back and you may be lucky to get a second flush of blooms. Lupin flowers come in a wide range of shades. Among the best are 'The Chatelaine', which has two-tone flowers in pink and white, and 'The Governor', which has purple and white flowers. Grey aphids that seem to attack the top of lupin shoots specifically may be a problem. Either squash them with your fingers or wash them off with a jet of soapy water.

tree lupin

Although technically a shrub, the tree lupin, *Lupinus arboreus*, is often seen in herbaceous borders. The flower spikes are shorter than on the perennial plants, but there are many, many more of them, all bright yellow and fragrant and borne over a long period in late spring to midsummer.

Lupinus hybrids

Lychnis Campion, Catchfly

There are several garden-worthy plants in this genus, all quite different in character, but all are easy to grow and providing long-lasting displays in the border.

Key features brilliant red flowers ∗ eye-catching ∗ good for hot-coloured borders ∗ hardy

Plant in full sun in any reasonable garden soil

Care feed and mulch in spring; add some supports as plants grow

Propagate by division or from seed in spring

Pests & diseases trouble-free

One of the most brilliant is the Jerusalem Cross or Maltese Cross, *Lychnis chalcedonica*. This is an upright plant, 90–120 x 30 cm (3–4 x 1 ft), with light green leaves, which set off the scarlet red flowers brilliantly. These are excellent plants for a hot-coloured border, especially when planted with golden-yellow achilleas (see page 38–9). They also look fabulous against a dark green yew hedge. A group of several plants will look better than a single one. They can be a bit floppy as they grow, so it is best to support them in some way.

contrast

A contrasting plant is dusty miller, *Lychnis coronaria*, 75 x 45 cm (30 x 18 in). This has silver-grey foliage and stems and brilliant magenta flowers. The foliage is hairy and a bit floppy, but it is a good foil for the flowers. Plants self-seed readily.

Lychnis chalcedonica

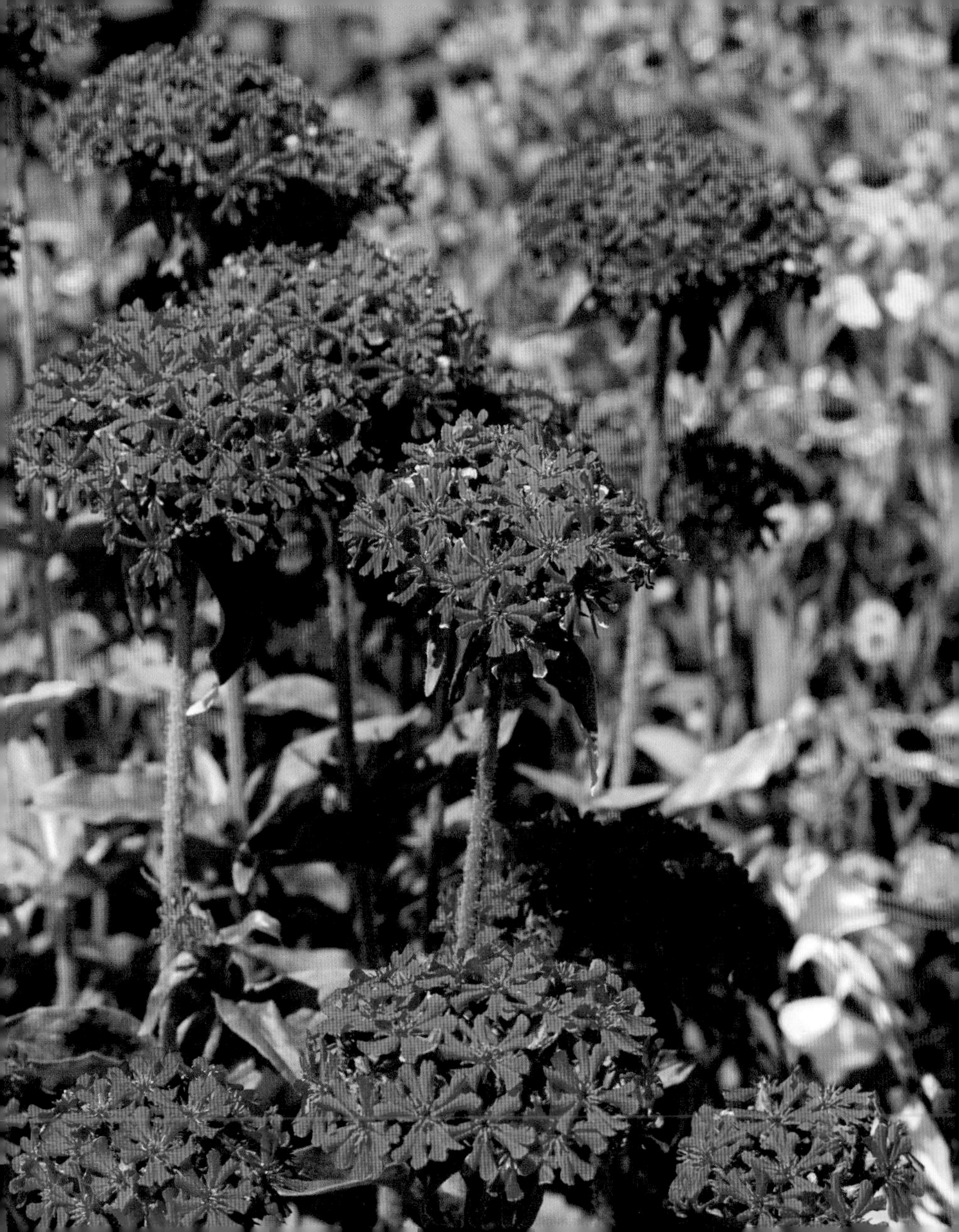

Lysimachia Loosestrife

Key features curiously shaped flowers * good conversation piece * quickly spreads * hardy

Plant in sun or light shade in any garden soil

Care dig around clumps to restrict them in spring; feed and mulch at the same time

Propagate by division in spring

Pests & diseases trouble-free

This is a varied genus with lots of interesting species to grow. One of the most curious of these, and always a conversation point, is *Lysimachia clethroides*, a tall, upright plant, to 1.2 m (4 ft), which does not need support. In mid- to late summer the small, star-like white flowers appear in spikes at the top of the plant, on stems that curve over a bit like a shepherd's crook.

L. ciliata, 120–160 cm (4–2 ft), has soft green leaves and yellow flowers in laxer heads. A drawback of these lysimachias is that if they like the conditions you offer they will spread rather rapidly. This is not a problem if you dig around them each spring and restrict their growth.

carpeter

In contrast to the taller species is the low, carpeting *L. nummularia* 'Aurea'. This has golden-yellow foliage and deeper yellow flowers. It spreads around at ground level and is excellent for filling in between other plants.

Lysimachia clethroides

Lythrum Purple Loosestrife

Key features eye-catching * self-supporting * clump-forming * good pond-side plant

Plant in full sun in damp spoil, but will grow in drier ground if it is rich in humus

Care feed and mulch in spring

Propagate by division in spring

Pests & diseases trouble-free

In spite of its common name, this is not related to the previous species. *Lythrum salicaria* is really a waterside plant, but it will grow in any properly prepared border.

It is a strongly growing, upright plant that needs no support. At the top of each stem is a spike of bright purple-pink flowers, which appear in late summer and continue into the autumn. Among the best cultivars are 'Blush' (pale pink), 'Robert' (bright pink) and 'Feuerkerze' (rose-red).

Unlike the yellow loosestrifes, the purple loosetrifes are better behaved and do not spread other than to make a decent-sized clump. Their 1.2 m (4 ft) stems look fabulous next to water, either a pond or stream, but are also useful in bog gardens.

more pinks

L. virgatum is similar to *L. salicaria*, but it is smaller, to 90 cm (3 ft) tall, and in some ways more elegant. The cultivars to look out for are 'Dropmore Purple' (deep pink-purple) and 'Rosy Gem' (rose-pink)

Lythrum salicaria

Macleaya Plume Poppy

Key features tall ∗ beautiful, subtle colour ∗ hardy

Plant in full sun in any reasonable garden soil

Care dig around the clump in spring to stop it spreading; feed and mulch at the same time

Propagate by division or from root cuttings in spring

Pests & diseases trouble-free

Although it is a member of the poppy family, the plants in this genus don't resemble the more familiar garden poppies at all. Plume poppies have tiny, coral-pink flowers, but their insignificance is more than made up for by the fact that they are carried in large plumes.

Macleaya cordata grows to 2.1–2.4 m (7–8 ft) tall. The undersides of the grey-green leaves are covered with white down and also have a coral tinge to them. To be really impressive you need a group of stems, but keep an eye on them because the group can turn into copse and then into a forest, so cut them back if necessary. They look good when planted along a wall or hedge.

better flowers

The cultivar 'Kelway's Coral Plume' is a form of *M. microcarpa*, but it is similar in stature and general appearance to *M. cordata*, with pinkish-bronze stems and leaves and a mass of tiny, coral-pink flowers borne in a large plume in early to midsummer.

Macleaya cordata

Meconopsis Meconopsis

Key features bright flowers ∗ good for shade or sun ∗ long season ∗ hardy

Plant in sun or shade in any soil, including the tops of walls

Care remove seedheads to prevent self-seeding

Propagate from seed sown in spring

Pests & diseases trouble-free

This genus contains one of the easiest plants to grow and also one of the most difficult. The easiest is the Welsh poppy, *Meconopsis cambrica*, a brightly coloured plant that is perfect for lightening a dark corner, where it will positively glow.

This is a relatively short plant, to 45 cm (18 in), with bright yellow or orange flowers, mainly borne in early summer but sporadically throughout the summer and autumn. For some reason it can be difficult to establish, but once it is happy it seeds freely. Because it self-seeds so readily it is important to deadhead after flowering.

blue poppies

Far more difficult to grow are the beautiful blue poppies, such as the Tibetan blue poppy, *M. betonificolia*, and the Himalayan blue poppy, *M. grandis*. These look fabulous in a woodland setting, but need a moist, maritime climate and humus-rich soil to perform at their best, and they prefer cool, damp summers.

Meconopsis cambrica

Monarda Bee Balm, Bergamot

Key features bright colours *
good in a drift * fragrant
foliage

Plant in full sun in rich, moist
soil

Care water in dry weather;
feed and mulch in spring

Propagate by division in
spring

Pests & diseases likely to get
mildew in dry summers, but it
does no harm and can be
ignored

These are good border plants, especially
when they are planted in drifts. The hooded
flowers are quite large and are carried in
whorls at the top of 1 m (3 ft) stems.

One of the oldest and still the best cultivars is _Monarda_
'Cambridge Scarlet'. This clump-forming plant has, as
its name suggests, bright scarlet flowers, borne from
midsummer to early autumn. The red monardas prefer
moist soil and tend to die out if they become too dry.
On the other hand, the taller, purple forms do better
in drier condition.

They are generally robust plants, but in more exposed
positions they may require some form of support.
The foliage is very fragrant, and it is a joy to weed
around them.

drifts of purple

There are several purple forms of monarda, and
these are generally long-lived plants. They grow
to 1–1.2 m (3–4 ft), but often have smaller
flowers than the red-flowered forms. Among the
best are 'Prärienacht' (dark purple) and
'Sagittarius' (lilac-pink).

Monarda didyma 'Cambridge Scarlet'

Nepeta Catmint

Key features fragrant foliage
* good for dry or gravel beds
* hardy

Plant in a sunny position in well-drained soil, but it will tolerate heavier conditions

Care feed and mulch in spring; cut to ground after flowering for new growth

Propagate by division or from basal cuttings in spring

Pests & diseases trouble-free

If you want a border that is a hazy mixture of soft pastel colours then you cannot ignore the catmints. The grey-green leaves have a distinctive minty fragrance, and most species are loved by cats.

There are several good plants to chose from, but one of the best is *Nepeta racemosa* 'Walker's Low', a typical catmint with airy stems clothed with lavender flowers over a long period in summer. It grows to about 35 cm (14 in) or more high. As the flowers begin to fade cut the stems back to the base and you will usually get a fresh flush of foliage and, usually, a new set of flowering stems. The foliage is an attractive silvery-grey.

All catmints make excellent specimens for a dry or gravel bed, although they will grow in quite heavy soil.

bright blue

Not all catmints are misty looking. *N. nervosa*, which grows to about 45 x 30 cm (18 x 12 in), bears spikes of purplish-blue flowers from midsummer to early autumn. It is not a long-lived plant but can be easily propagated from basal cuttings (see page 31).

Nepeta nervosa

Origanum Marjoram

Key features masses of flowers * fragrant foliage * good for dry and gravel beds * late-flowering

Plant in sun in reasonably well-drained soil, although they will tolerate heavier ground

Care feed and mulch in spring; cut back after flowering to prevent self-seeding

Propagate by division in spring

Pests & diseases trouble-free

This lovely dual-purpose plant looks attractive in the border, and the leaves can be used as a herb in the kitchen. There are a surprising number of *origanums* to chose from, but they all have aromatic leaves and small pink or mauve flowers.

For the main border one of the forms of *Origanum laevigatum* would be a good choice, and 'Herrenhausen', 45 cm (18 in) tall, and 'Hopleys', 60 cm (24 in) tall, are two of the best. These are upright plants, with purplish stems, and they produce masses of tiny purple flowers from late summer onwards. The only snag with these beautiful plants is that they will self-seed prodigiously, so deadhead after flowering so you do not have to remove unwanted seedlings.

front of border

There are some lovely plants for the front of the border. 'Kent Beauty' is possibly the best representative of this group. It grows to 30 cm (12 in) high and has masses of greenish-pink flowers that look like tiny hops.

Origanum laevigatum

Paeonia Peony

Key features colourful * good foliage * enormous choice of cultivars * hardy

Plant in full sun in any reasonable garden soil; do not plant too deep

Care feed and mulch in spring

Propagate by division in spring or from seed in autumn

Pests & diseases trouble-free

This is one of the glories of the herbaceous border. First, there is the beautiful emerging foliage, which often takes on purple or bronze hues. Then there are the fantastic flowers in white, pink or red, some double, some single, and finally there are the colours of the autumn foliage and the seedpods. This is a plant that gives value for money.

There are thousands of named herbaceous peonies to choose from, but *Paeonia officinalis* may be a good place to start. It has simple, single flowers, which are bright red or rose-pink in early to midsummer. Don't plant peonies too deeply – just to the level it comes in the pot. It may take a couple of years to start to bloom.

earliest peony

The almost unpronounceable *P. mlokosewitschii*, the Caucasian peony, or Molly the Witch as she is affectionately known, bears bright yellow flowers in late spring or early summer and has superb, blue-green foliage and wonderful seedpods. It's a fantastic plant, growing to 70–90 cm (28–36 in) tall and across.

Paeonia officinalis

Papaver Poppy

Key features colourful * easy to grow * good for dry and gravel beds * hardy

Plant in full sun in any garden soil

Care feed and mulch in spring; cut to the ground after flowering

Propagate from root cuttings in early winter or by division in spring

Pests & diseases trouble-free

Including perennial poppies in a mixed border is a great way of introducing bright colours. The individual flowers last for only a few days, but as one fades another opens.

Papaver orientale in all its many cultivars is the main poppy for the herbaceous border. It forms a clump of rough-textured basal leaves, from which rise stems to 45 cm (18 in) or more carrying large, papery flowers in brilliant reds or oranges in early summer. There are now a lot of more subtle colours to choose from, including 'Patty's Plum' (plum-mauve), 'Turkish Delight' (pink) and 'Mrs Perry' (salmon-pink).

Alas, once they have flowered they look untidy, so grow other plants in front to hide them and cut them down to ground level to get new, better foliage.

rural simplicity

Most of the poppies of agricultural land are annuals, but *P. lateritium* is similar in its simplicity. It is a small plant, 40 x 30 cm (16 x 12 in), with thin stems rising above the foliage, bearing a long succession of dark orange flowers in mid- to late summer.

Papaver orientale 'Cedric's Pink'

Penstemon Penstemon

Key features colourful * long season * easy to propagate * makes good drifts

Plant in full sun in any reasonable garden soil

Care feed and mulch in spring, at the same time cutting down the previous year's stems

Propagate from cuttings at any time of year

Pests & diseases trouble-free

This is a good plant for first-time gardeners because it is both easy to grow and easy to propagate. They are also wonderfully colourful plants, to 60 cm (24 in) tall, making them suitable for the middle of the border and even for bedding schemes. The erect stems carry light to medium green leaves.

There are many named cultivars to choose from, most of which flower over a long period from midsummer to early or mid-autumn. The delightful 'Evelyn' bears rose-pink flowers that are paler pink inside and marked with deeper pink lines. Penstemons are hardy, although those with the biggest flowers tend to be slightly less so. It is best, therefore, to leave the old stems on the plants until spring to protect the crowns from frost. They are sturdy plants and do not need support except in very exposed positions.

bright red

If you want a really bright patch of colour choose 'Andenken an Friedrich Hahn', which is sometimes sold as 'Garnet'. It produces large, beautiful, wine red flowers.

Penstemon 'Hidcote Pink'

Persicaria Knotweed

Key features good groundcover * long season * colourful * good in drifts * hardy

Plant in sun in any garden soil

Care feed and mulch in spring; dig round plants if necessary to control their growth

Propagate by division in spring

Pests & diseases trouble-free

The knotweeds have had a bad press because of some of the more rampant members of the group. However, there are many garden-worthy plants in this group, which are not only well behaved but which form the backbone of the herbaceous border.

Bistort, *P. amplexicaulis*, is one of those useful plants. It forms a large clump, 1 m (3 ft) high, of relatively coarse leaves above which rise masses of thin stems of narrow spikes of tiny flowers from midsummer to early autumn. Most cultivars have red flowers, but there are also pink and white versions. They do spread a little but can easily be cut back to their original position and are not invasive.

colourful carpet

A good groundcover plant for the front of a border is *P. affinis*, which gets to about 25 cm (10 in) tall. The dark green foliage turns reddish-bronze in autumn, and from midsummer to early autumn it bears spikes of rose-pink and red flowers. It will form a colourful carpet but is not invasive or thuggish.

Persicaria amplexicaulis

Phlox Phlox

Key features elegant * easy to grow * scented * good cut flowers * hardy

Plant in full sun in any reasonable garden soil

Care feed and mulch in spring

Propagate from root cuttings in early winter

Pests & diseases eelworms

This is another traditional cottage-garden plant, but it also has its place in the modern border. It forms tall stems, to 1.5 m (5 ft) or more in some forms, that carry clusters of flat flowers, in white and various shades of pink, mauve and purple, some subtle, others quite bright. Many are perfumed.

Phlox paniculata and its cultivars, which bloom from summer to mid-autumn, all make self-supporting clumps that rarely need any staking. All phloxes occasionally suffer from infestations of eelworms (microscopic nematodes), which distort the foliage. There is nothing you can do about this except burn the plants. Always buy from reputable nurseries and increase your stock by root cuttings rather than division, because the eelworms are not found in the roots.

woodland phlox

Phlox divaricata and its cultivars is a good plant for woodland beds. It grows to about 30 cm (12 in) high and has airy stems and typical phlox flowers that are pale violet-blue, lavender-blue or white. It like a humus-rich, woodland soil.

Phlox paniculata 'Glamis'

Phormium New Zealand Flax

Key features imposing * good focal point * interesting foliage and flowers * hardy

Plant in full sun in any garden soil

Care feed and mulch in spring; at the same time remove old flower stalks and any dead leaves

Propagate by division in spring

Pests & diseases trouble-free

If you want a really striking plant as a focal point then this may be it. *Phormium tenax* forms a great fountain of yellow-green, sword-like leaves that arch out from the centre of the clump, which grows to 1.5 m (5 ft) or more across. Then, in the late summer or autumn huge flower stalks, to 3 m (10 ft) high, shoot up from the centre of the foliage, bearing red flowers

Phormiums can be planted in a mixed border or used on their own as a specimen in the centre of a lawn or a gravel bed, for example. Think carefully about the position before you plant, because established phormiums are difficult to move.

something smaller

Some of the cultivars of *P. cookianum* and some hybrids are much smaller than *P. tenax* and these are more suitable for smaller gardens. Look out for 'Bronze Baby', a hybrid of *P. tenax*, which grows to about 80 cm (32 in) high and across and has bronze-green leaves.

Phormium tenax

Polemonium Jacob's Ladder

Key features good early-summer plant * attractive foliage * can be used as cut flowers * hardy

Plant in light shade or full sun in any reasonable garden soil

Care feed and mulch in spring; remove flower stems before seeding

Propagate from seed or by division in spring

Pests & diseases trouble-free

Polemonium caeruleum is known as Jacob's ladder because the leaves resemble an old pole ladder, with a central stem and leaflets on either side at right angles to the stem. As well as attractive foliage, it has open bell-shaped, clear blue flowers in spring.

These are upright plants, growing to 60–90 cm (2–3 ft) tall and about 30 cm (12 in) across. The plants are not long lived, but usually produce enough seedlings to provide you with new plants every two or three years. If you want to keep these under control, cut off the flowers stalks immediately after flowering.

soft spring

In contrast, *P. carneum* bears soft mauve bell-shaped flowers on a delightful jumble of airy stems in early summer. Plants grow 20–40 cm (8–16 in) tall and only 20 cm (8 in) across.

Polemonium caeruleum

Polygonatum Solomon's Seal

Key features tranquil-looking plant * good woodlander * good cut flowers * hardy

Plant in light shade in humus-rich soil

Care feed and mulch in early spring

Propagate by division after flowering

Pests & diseases hand pick sawflies in midsummer

There is something very tranquil and peaceful about this plant. It is a woodlander, and in the soft greenish light under the trees this graceful plant, with its arching stems and pairs of white bells hanging beneath each pair of leaves, can look superb.

Polygonatum x *hybridum* and its various cultivars can be grown in sun, but they do best when grown in light shade, and in a small garden a position under deciduous shrubs would be suitable. Plants grow slowly, eventually getting to 60–120 cm (2–3 ft) high. The little white flowers appear in late spring, and they are followed by small black fruits. The cultivar 'Striatum' has cream-striped leaves.

whorled

A good variation of the ordinary Solomon's seal is *P. verticilliatum*, known as whorled Solomon's seal. This is a more upright plant, to 90 cm (3 ft) tall, with whorls of narrow leaves at intervals up the stem and with slightly smaller, greenish-white flowers hanging below them.

Polygonatum x *hybridum*

Potentilla Cinquefoil, Potentilla

Key features good gap filler ∗ quiet presence ∗ long flowering season ∗ hardy

Plant in sun in any garden soil

Care feed and mulch in spring

Propagate from seed sown in spring

Pests & diseases trouble-free

This is a large genus of which the best known members are perhaps the shrubs derived from *Potentilla fruticosa*, but it also includes a large number of herbaceous plants, mainly with yellow or red flowers.

P. recta, up to 60 cm (2 ft), which has pale yellow flowers, is the parent of some of the best of the yellow-flowered plants. 'Warrenii', for example, has vivid yellow flowers opening from hairy buds, and *P. recta* var. *sulphurea* has creamy yellow blooms. These plants have an upright habit, and they will climb through other plants. They flower over a long period from early to late summer, and although they self-seed readily, unwanted seedlings are easy to remove.

coloured forms

Himalayan cinquefoil, *P. atrosanguinea*, bears very bright red flowers from summer to early autumn, and *P. nepalensis*, which produces scarlet flowers, has several interesting cultivars, 'Miss Willmott', which bears rose-pink flowers with a dark red centre, and 'Roxana', which has bright orange flowers.

Potentilla recta

Primula Primula

Key features scented ✴ early-flowering ✴ good cut flowers ✴ hardy

Plant in sun or light shade in any garden soil as long as it is moisture-retentive

Care feed and mulch in spring

Propagate by division or from seed in spring

Pests & diseases sparrows may pick off the flowerheads

This is a very large genus, containing a wide range of plants, nearly all of which are garden-worthy. One of the best species of the group, mainly because of its placid simplicity, is _Primula vulgaris_, the primrose.

This delightful plant grows to only about 15 cm (6 in) high, and it forms a posy of mid-green leaves from which erupt many pale yellow flowers in spring. It will grow in sun or shade, although it does prefer moist but not waterlogged soil. It sometimes self-sows, but who cares with such a marvellous plant?

candelabras

Some members of the genus are known as candelabra primulas because they produce several whorls of flowers in tiers on robust, erect stems. _P. japonicum_ has reddish-purple flowers. Candelabra primulas look particularly attractive near ponds or streams.

Primula Polyanthus Group

Pulmonaria Lungwort

These are useful dual-purpose plants: not only do they have good flowers in spring, but once these are over they become a good foliage plant for the rest of the year.

Key features good flowers in late winter and spring * good foliage plant * hardy

Plant in light shade in any reasonable garden soil

Care feed and mulch in early spring; remove flowers and leaves after flowering

Propagate by division after flowering

Pests & diseases trouble-free

Nearly all pulmonarias have the same flower and leaf type. The flowers are small funnels, usually blue, which change to pink or red as the flowers age, but there are also pink, red and white forms. *Pulmonaria* 'Lewis Palmer', for example, has pink flowers that age to blue, while 'Sissinghurst White' has white flowers that open from pink buds. The foliage is bristly and may be oval or long, almost strap-like. Some pulmonarias have plain green leaves, but other forms have leaves that are splashed with silver. Once the flowers have died back in late spring, shear off the whole plant and you will be rewarded with a fresh crop of leaves that will make a good foliage plant for the rest of the year.

blue cowslip

P. angustifolia, which grows to 30 cm (12 in) or more, bears deep blue flowers from early to late spring. The attractive leaves are plain dark green. These plants do best in light shade.

Pulmonaria 'Diana Clare'

Ranunculus Buttercup

Key features easy to grow
* early-flowering * good cut
flowers * hardy

Plant in sun in moist soil

Care feed and mulch in
spring; cut back after
flowering

Propagate from seed sown
soon after it is ripe

Pests & diseases trouble-free

Most gardeners spend a lot of time removing
buttercups from the garden, but there are
several plants within the genus that are
welcome additions to perennial borders.

Ranunculus aconitifolius is an airy plant, with lots of
white, buttercup-shaped flowers, held high on waving
stems above the glossy, dark green foliage. The double
form, 'Flore Pleno', which is known as the Fair Maids of
Kent or Fair Maids of France, is the same as the
species except for the double flowers. The flowers are
borne in late spring into early summer, and the plants
do best in damp soil.

celandines

R. ficaria, the common celandine, is often
regarded as a weed, although the pretty yellow
flowers appear in early spring when little else is in
bloom. The flowers and leaves die back after
flowering and are not a nuisance, although plants
will spread and can be invasive. There are several
cultivars, which are less invasive, including double
forms such as 'Double Bronze' and 'Double Mud',
as well as some, such as 'Salmon's White', with
coloured and patterned foliage.

Ranunculus aconitifolius

Rodgersia Rodgersia

Key features wonderful foliage * spectacular flowers * forms good clumps * hardy

Plant in moist soil in light shade or sun

Care feed and mulch in early spring

Propagate by division in spring

Pests & diseases trouble-free

This is a genus of beautiful plants that deserve to be better known, both for their attractive foliage and for their flowers. They do best in reliably damp soil and are sometimes included in bog gardens.

Rodgersia aesculifolia is one of the best species. This grows to 1.2 m (4 ft) or more tall, with large, fluffy heads of cream-pink flowers in midsummer. The leaves are shaped like those of the horse chestnut, _Aesculus hippocastanum_, a fact that is reflected in the plant's botanical name, and they have a bronzy tint to their undulating surface, which reflects the light well. This is an ideal plant for a damp, lightly shaded spot, although it will also grow in sun as long as the soil does not dry out. They are strong enough to need no support.

pink flowers

R. pinnata is also a beautiful plant, similar in many ways to _R. aesculifolia_, although it is shorter, reaching only 1 m (3 ft). It is seen at its best in the form 'Superba', which has bright pink flowers in mid- to late summer. The lovely 'Alba' has white flowers.

Rodgersia pinnata

Rudbeckia Cone Flower

Key features long flowering season * forms good drifts * good cut flowers * hardy

Plant in full sun, preferably in moisture-retentive soil

Care feed and mulch in spring; cut back plants that spread too far

Propagate by division in spring

Pests & diseases trouble-free

In late summer and autumn herbaceous borders are often dominated by yellow flowers, but *Rudbeckia fulgida* var. *deamii* is one of those plants that would be missed if were not there. It is a member of the daisy family, bearing flowers with golden-yellow petals and a brown, domed central disc over an extraordinarily long period from late summer to mid-autumn.

It spreads to make a large clump, 60 cm (2 ft), but the sturdy stems need no support. Established plants may need to be restricted to keep them in check, but they are not invasive. If the soil becomes too dry the leaves begin to wilt, but quickly recover when watered.

large daisies

There are some spectacularly tall species in the genus. *R. lacinata*, for example, grows to 2.1 m (7 ft) tall, topped with pale, green-yellow flowers with a darker green-yellow central disc from midsummer to mid-autumn. It may need support in exposed places.

Rudbeckia hirta

Salvia Sage

Key features bright blues and purples ∗ flowers over long period ∗ good for gravel beds

Plant in full sun in any reasonable garden soil; does best in free-draining soil

Care feed and mulch in spring

Propagate from cuttings in spring

Pests & diseases trouble-free

The genus is probably best known for the herb *Salvia officinalis* but it also contains many attractive garden plants, including annuals and shrubs as well as a good many herbaceous perennials.

One of the best perennials is *S. nemorosa*, which forms a low bush, to 60 cm (2 ft) or more high and the same across, with long spikes of flowers in various shades of blue and purple, sometimes white or pink, in summer. There are several cultivars, including 'Amethyst' (purplish-blue), 'Ostfriesland' (dark violet-blue) and 'Lubecca' (violet surrounded by purplish-red bracts). They will grow on most soils but prefer well-drained conditions and tend to be short-lived on heavier ground. They are ideal for gravel beds.

spectacular salvia

A short-lived but spectacular salvia, especially in damp soil, is *S. sclarea* var. *turkestanica*. This grows to 1–1.5 m (3–5 ft) tall and has large, sticky leaves, to 23 cm (9 in) long, and spikes of very large flowers that are a delicate combination of white, blue and pink.

Salvia involucrata 'Bethellii'

Scabiosa Pincushion Flower, Scabious

Key features good for pastel-coloured borders * good cut flowers * hardy

Plant in sun in any reasonable garden soil

Care feed and mulch in spring

Propagate by division in spring

Pests & diseases trouble-free

It is important to balance the brightly coloured plants with a few subtler, more restrained ones, and scabious are an ideal choice for this purpose.

The soft flowers of *Scabiosa caucasica* float gently above the greyish-green, finely cut foliage in mid- to late summer. Plants grow to about 60 cm (2 ft), but the airy, floating stems and flowers make this a suitable plant for the front as well as the middle of a border. The flowers are mainly pale blue or lavender-blue.

over the top

Once classified as a Scabious, but now moved off, is the closely related *Cephalaria gigantea*. This a tall plant, 2.1 m (7 ft) or more, with cushion-like flowers of pale yellow. A good back of border plant.

Scabiosa caucasica 'Clive Graves'

Sedum Stonecrop

Key features colourful * late season * attracts bees * hardy

Plant in full sun in any reasonable garden soil

Care feed and mulch in spring

Propagate by division in spring or from leaf cuttings in summer

Pests & diseases trouble-free

Sedums are instantly recognizable in the garden because they are succulents – that is, they have fleshy leaves. It is a large genus, containing plants that are only a couple of centimetres high as well as some that grow to 60 cm (2 ft) or more.

Sedum spectabile and its many cultivars are typical of the taller sedums. Known as ice plants because of their ice-green foliage, they have large flat heads in late summer and autumn of pink or red flowers that are much visited by butterflies and bees. 'Iceberg' has paler leaves than the species and white flowers, and 'Brilliant' has vivid pink flowers. They will grow in most soils but are especially suitable for dry and gravel beds.

purple foliage

A good alternative to *S. spectabile* is *S. telephium*. This is also an upright plant, with similar leaves and flowerheads. The form *S. telephium* subsp. *maximum* 'Atropurpureum' has striking purplish stems and leaves and deep pinkish-red flowers.

Sedum spectabile

Sidalcea False Mallow, Prairie Mallow

Key features elegant *
beautiful pink flowers * hardy

Plant in sun in any reasonable
garden soil

Care feed and mulch in spring

Propagate by division in
spring

Pests & diseases trouble-free

As a contrast to plants with their feet planted
firmly on the ground it is useful to add plants
that are airy and light. *Sidalceas* are not as
light and floating as some, but the pink
flowers still have that quality of floating
above others in the border. If anything, these
plants resemble a miniature hollyhock.

Sidalcea malviflora, which grows to about 1.2 m (4 ft)
tall, bears pink, shallow cup-shaped flowers in early to
midsummer, set off by the mid-green foliage. One of
the prettiest forms is 'Elsie Heugh', which has pale pink
flowers, each of which is delicately fringed. The flowers
of 'Reverend Page Roberts' are a pale rose-pink.

white alternative

S. candida is similar to *S. malviflora*, but in mid-
to late summer it bears stunning white flowers,
accentuated by a central boss of crimson. It is
slightly shorter at 1 m (3 ft).

Sidalcea malviflora

Silene Campion, Catchfly

Key features good front-of-border plant * colourful * late-flowering * hardy

Plant in sun in any reasonable garden soil

Care mulch in spring

Propagate by division in spring

Pests & diseases trouble-free

There are hundreds of species in this genus, and in the wild they can be found in a wide range of habitats. There will, therefore, be a campion that is suitable for the conditions you can offer in your garden.

The clump-forming *Silene schafta*, 25 cm (10 in), is a good choice for the front of border, the bright green leaves and deep magenta flowers adding a splash of colour from late summer to autumn. The flowers have long tubes, which end in an array of splayed-out, notched petals. A good form is 'Shell Pink', which has delicately pale pink flowers.

fringed white

A good campion for the spring garden is *S. fimbriata*, which grows to 60 cm (2 ft) tall. Each of the white flowers has an attractive fringe around the edge of the petals.

Silene uniflora

Sisyrinchium Sisyrinchium

Key features striking in a group ∗ provides plenty of self-sown seedlings ∗ hardy

Plant in full sun in any reasonable garden soil

Care feed and mulch in spring; remove blackened leaves; cut off stems after flowering to prevent self-seeding

Propagate by division or from seed in spring

Pests & diseases trouble-free

Many gardeners have something of a love-hate relationship with *Sisyrinchium striatum*. They hate it because it self-seeds so prolifically, although the excess seedlings are easy to remove, but they love it for the wonderful creamy yellow flowers that appear in early to midsummer.

The grey-green, sword-shaped foliage is arranged in a fan, much in the manner of flag irises. From these arise tall stems of funnel-shaped flowers, which shut at night. Each plant is up to 60 cm (2 ft) tall. The tips of the leaves turn black in winter and should be removed. Renew the clumps by dividing them every so often to keep the plants fresh or allow seedlings to grow on.

variegation

There is a lovely variegated form of this plant, 'Aunt May', which has grey-green leaves, down which run creamy yellow stripes. Unfortunately, it is not as vigorous as the species, but if you divide clumps regularly it can be kept going easily.

Sisyrinchium striatum

Smilacina False Spikenard

Key features good for a white border * fragrant * good cut flowers * attractive foliage * hardy

Plant in light shade in any reasonable garden soil

Care feed and mulch in spring; dig around clumps in spring to control invasive shoots

Propagate by division in spring

Pests & diseases trouble-free

This is a close relative of Solomon's seal, *Polygonatum* (see pages 190–91), but instead of bells it bears frothy clusters of creamy white flowers in late spring to early summer. These make a good contrast to the green leaves.

Smilacina racemosa gradually spreads to form a decent-sized clump, to 75 cm (30 in), but it is not invasive, and excess growth can be easily removed. It does best in a partially shaded position, but because the flowers are wonderfully scented it is worth finding a space near the front of a border where the fragrance can be easily appreciated.

smaller relative

Less often seen is *S. stellata*, which is sometimes known as star-flowered lily-of-the-valley. It is smaller, at about 60 cm (24 in) tall, and produces a sprinkling of attractive small, starry flowers, which are followed by red berries. It is ideal for a wild garden but can be invasive if not kept under control.

Smilacina racemosa

Solidago Golden Rod

Key features good colour for late summer ∗ makes a good drift ∗ good cut flowers ∗ hardy

Plant in sun in any reasonable garden soil

Care feed and mulch in spring

Propagate by division in spring

Pests & diseases trouble-free

These are excellent plants for cheering up flagging late-summer and early-autumn borders at a time when other plants are beginning to go over. The feathery clusters of small, golden-yellow flowers wave in the breeze on strong, erect stems.

The cultivars are far better in the garden than any of the species, which can be both rather coarse and invasive. *Solidago* 'Goldenmosa', for example, grows to about 75 cm (30 in) tall, and the tiny, bright yellow flowers are borne in large sprays to 30 cm (12 in) long. Even taller is 'Golden Wings', which will reach 2 m (6 ft). All the cultivars will grow in most soils and spread to make a decent clump without being invasive.

mixed with asters

There is a hybrid between *Solidago* and *Aster*, appropriately named *Solidaster*. This produces plants similar to ordinary golden rod, but the heads are more lemony in colour, with individual flowers being slightly larger. It is well worth growing, especially in the form 'Lemore'.

Solidago 'Goldengate'

Stachys Betony, Stachys, Woundwort

This genus provides many good plants for our gardens. They are mainly grown for their flowers, but one of them, *Stachys byzantina*, is prized for its foliage.

Key features silver foliage ∗ good groundcover ∗ good for gravel beds ∗ hardy

Plant in full sun in any reasonable soil

Care feed and mulch in spring; cut back if extending beyond its allotted space

Propagate by division in spring

Pests & diseases trouble-free

Lambs' ears is a good descriptive name for the leaves, which form a carpet of rather floppy grey-green 'ears', all covered with silver-grey hairs. It does flower, with stems rising to 45 cm (18 in) above the ground in summer. These stems are also clothed in silvery hairs and bear half-hidden pink flowers. Some gardeners cut these off, preferring to keep this as a foliage plant, but others find a quiet charm in the flowers. It is a valuable edging plant for the front of a border and is a useful filler between other plants.

purple heads

In contrast, *S. macrantha*, 30 cm (12 in), is grown for its flowers, which appear in early summer and last into early autumn. They are carried on the top of upright stalks and form domes of bright purple. The cultivar 'Superba' has dark pink-purple flowers.

Stachys macrantha

Thalictrum Meadow Rue

Key features tall, back-of-the-border plants * good flowers * good foliage * hardy

Plant in sun in any garden soil

Care feed and mulch in spring. Support if necessary.

Propagate by division in spring or from seed sown soon after it is set

Pests & diseases trouble-free

Tall, back-of-the-border plants are always useful, but most tend to flower quite late in the season as they need time to grow. *Thalictrum flavum* subsp. *glaucum*, however, manages to grow to 2.1 m (7 ft) by midsummer. It is a doubly attractive plant as it has both good flowers and foliage.

The acid yellow flowers are tiny and are borne in fluffy heads on tall, sturdy stems. They are set off by glaucous, grey-green foliage. Once the flowers are over they can be cut off, leaving the rest of the plant as a foliage plant until the leaves, too, begin to fade. In exposed positions the stems may need supporting with canes.

spring flowers

Another striking meadow rue is *T. aquilegifolium*, which grows to 90 cm (3 ft). From late spring to early summer it produces wonderfully fluffy heads of light purple or white flowers. These are followed by seeds, which hang like hundreds of earrings, making this an altogether most attractive and unusual plant.

Thalictrum flavum subsp. *glaucum*

Trollius Globeflower

Key features bright and cheerful * suitable for boggy ground * good as cut flowers * hardy

Plant in a sunny position in moist soil

Care feed and mulch in spring

Propagate by division in spring

Pests & diseases trouble-free

Trollius x *cultorum* is a cheerful plant to brighten up spring and early summer borders. The flowers in cultivated forms are large globes, 3–4 cm (1¼–1½ in) across, in shades of yellow or gold. Their resemblance to their close relative the buttercup can easily be seen in the flowers.

In the wild the species *T. europaeus* is found in boggy ground, and these are the conditions that globeflowers prefer in cultivation, although they will grow in any garden soil that does not dry out too much. They look particularly good in bog gardens next to water. Unlike many buttercups, they are not in the least invasive.

golden globes

T. pumilus is a much smaller form, 30 cm (12 in), which is suitable for a site that can be kept reliably damp, such as beside a pond or stream. The golden-yellow flowers, which appear from late spring to early summer, open more widely than those of its larger cousins.

Trollius x *cultorum* 'Feuertroll'

Verbascum Mullein

Key features stately ∗ good vertical emphasis ∗ good for gravel beds ∗ hardy

Plant in full sun in any reasonable garden soil

Care feed and mulch in spring

Propagate from seed sown in spring

Pests & diseases mullein moths, which munch the leaves, should be picked off by hand

The tall, candelabra-shaped mulleins, such as *Verbascum bombyciferum*, have a valuable place in the perennial border but they are biennials, so are outside our scope. *V. chaixii*, however, is a smaller perennial version and is well worth considering.

These mulleins grow to 1 m (3 ft) or more and have the same long stems covered with yellow flowers as the biennials. The pale yellow flowers, which are borne from mid- to late summer, have a purple eye. These plants have taproots and once established are difficult to move, so consider their position carefully before planting. They are suitable for growing in dry and gravel beds.

colourful cousins

Several perennial hybrids based on purple mullein, *V. phoeniceum*, make attractive and easy-to-grow border plants. They have been given names that are largely descriptive of the flowers, which are borne in late spring to early summer, including 'Flush of Pink', 'Rosetta' and 'Violetta'.

Verbascum phoeniceum

Verbena Verbena

Key features tall and wiry * long-lasting flowers * easy to grow

Plant in sun in any reasonable garden soil

Care feed and mulch in spring

Propagate from seed in spring

Pests & diseases trouble-free

One of the most spectacular plants of the late summer and autumn is *Verbena bonariensis*, which has become popular in recent years, both for its height and for its purple flowers.

These are tall plants, to 2 m (6 ft) or more high and about 45 cm (18 in) across, but the upright stems are so slender and airy that they are often planted near the front of the border, allowing glimpses through them of the other plants behind. The purple flowers, which appear from midsummer to early autumn, are borne in clusters on the open, branching stems. The sturdy stems need no support, and plants will self-seed.

more substance

The clump-forming *V. hastata*, 1 m (3 ft) high and 60 cm (24 in) across, is a different type of plant, still upright but somehow more solid, with the stems clothed in light green leaves. From early summer to early autumn clusters of pink-purple flowers are borne on the ends of the stems. There are also white and pink forms.

Verbena bonariensis

Veronica Speedwell, Veronica

Key features quietly impressive * soft blue flowers * front-of-border plant * hardy

Plant in sun or part shade in moisture-retentive soil

Care feed and mulch in spring; cut off spikes after flowering

Propagate by division in spring

Pests & diseases trouble-free

This large genus contains many good garden plants. One quiet plant that is not at all overpowering is *Veronica gentianoides*. This has ground-level shiny green leaves from which rise 45 cm (18 in) stems bearing spikes of pale blue.

It is an excellent plant for the front of a border, especially in a scheme based on pastel colours. The species itself is so beautiful that it is scarcely worth looking for the cultivars, of which there are several. There is a white form, *V. gentianoides* 'Alba', but it is rather disappointing, with flowers that are not pure white, more of a dirty grey. There is also a variegated form, 'Variegata', which has white-variegated leaves. It prefers a moist soil and wilts rapidly in dry conditions.

carpets of colour

Another front of border plant is *Veronica spicata* whose foliage is not at all glossy. It spreads to form a small mat but is not invasive. There are plenty of cultivars to explore, the majority of which are shades of blue, but there are pink and white versions as well.

Veronica gentianoides

Viola Viola

Key features delightful ∗ good front-of-border plants ∗ easy to grow ∗ hardy

Plant in light shade in moist soil

Care feed and mulch in early spring

Propagate from basal cuttings in spring

Pests & diseases slugs can kill a plant

The genus *Viola* has three groups of useful plants as far as the gardener is concerned. The biggest are the pansies, the smallest the violets and in between are the violas. There is now a large number of hybrid violas in a wide range of colours.

One of the most delightful is 'Molly Sanderson', which has such dark purple flowers that it looks almost black. This is an exquisite little plant, which, like all other violas, prefers a position out of the hottest sun and in a soil that doesn't dry out. They should be planted in the front of the border, where they will grow to about 20 cm (8 in) high. They are not long-lived plants but can easily be increased from basal cuttings (see page 31 for propagation).

winter sweet

Sweet violets, *Viola odorata*, are always worth growing, and they can easily be tucked under deciduous shrubs in ground that would otherwise be bare. The deliciously scented flowers appear in late winter and early spring. The flowers are usually violet-blue, but there are other shades of blue as well as white, pink and red.

Viola 'Molly Sanderson'

Zantedeschia Arum Lily, White Arum

Key features dramatic flowers * excellent by or in water * good cut flowers

Plant in sun preferably in moist or wet soil

Care feed and mulch in spring; give winter protection in colder areas

Propagate by division in spring

Pests & diseases slugs

Some gardeners prefer not to grow these plants because they associate the unusual flowers with funerals, but they make interesting and excellent garden plants.

Zantedeschia aethiopica is the most widely grown plant and it has wonderful, pure white spathes in late spring to midsummer, which emerge from glossy, dark green foliage. They will grow to 1 m (3 ft) or more tall. They do best in damp soil, and they are, in fact, often grown in the margins of a pond in water about 30 cm (12 in) deep, when they are protected from frost and slugs. Most forms are now hardy in ordinary garden soil (as long as it does not dry out). The cultivar 'Crowborough' is supposedly the hardiest of the cultivars.

yellow spathes

Another species that is becoming more frequently seen is the golden arum, *Z. elliottiana*. This has bright yellow spathes, and the large, dark green leaves are covered with fine white spots. This definitely requires protection from the frost.

Zantedeschia aethiopica

index

Page numbers in *italics* refer to illustrations

acknowledgements

Publisher Jane Birch
Editor Ruth Wiseall
Executive art editor Sally Bond
Designer Joanna MacGregor
Picture research manager Guilia Hetherington
Senior production controller Amanda Mackie

photography

Alamy /Blickwinkel 99, 121, 149; /David Noton Photography 27; /floralpick 209; /Flowerphotos 55; /Holmes Garden Photos 7, 17, 49, 165, 187, 205, 235; /Jim Allan 189; /John Glover 15, 191; /Jonathan Need 125; /Mark Bolton 105; /Mark Milward 81; /Martin Hughes-Jones 215; /Neil Homes 57; /Niall McDiarmid 145, 213, 229; /Organica 223; /Photofrenetic 137; /Sharon Koch 14; /Steffen Hauser/botanikfoto 173; /Tom Viggars 67.

Corbis UK Ltd /Clay Perry 85; /Mark Bolton 93.

Garden World Images 19; /Trevor Sims 211; /Ashley Biddle 119, /Charles Hawes 13, /Debbie Jolliff 115; /Gilles Delacroix 12, 135, 155, 167, 171; /Isabelle Anderson 10; /Jenny Lilly 32; /Lee Thomas 11; /Mark Bolton 109; /Martin Hughes-Jones 123, 133, 139, 141, 163, 197; /Mein Schoener Garten 30; /N+R Colborn 63; /Rita Coates 51, 151, 217; /Rodger Tamblyn 16, 65, 161; /Sine Chesterman 33; /Trevor Sims 47, 59, 77, 147, 153, 183.

Gap Photos /Adrian Bloom 201; /Friedrich Strauss 89; /Mark Bolton 199; /Richard Bloom 233; /Visions 175, 192.

Octopus Publishing Group Limited 37, 39, 41, 45, 61, 69, 71, 73, 75, 79, 87, 91, 97, 101, 107, 113, 117, 127, 131, 143, 159, 169, 179, 194, 203, 207, 221, 225, 227, 181, 231.

Photolibrary 177; /Friedrich Strauss 23, 24; /Jo Whitworth 156; /Linda Burgess 21; /Mark Bolton 29; /Michael Davis 53; /Steffen Hauser 83; /Stephen Henderson 103; /Susie Mccaffrey 185.

Shutterstock 95, 111; /Joanne van Hoof 43; /Steve Fellers 219.